HOW TO THINK LIKE SHAKESPEARE

HOW TO
THINK
LIKE SHAKESPEARE

LESSONS FROM A RENAISSANCE EDUCATION

SCOTT NEWSTOK

PRINCETON UNIVERSITY PRESS

PRINCETON AND OXFORD

Published by Princeton University Press
41 William Street, Princeton, New Jersey 08540
6 Oxford Street, Woodstock, Oxfordshire OX20 1TR

press.princeton.edu

Library of Congress Cataloging-in-Publication Data

Names: Newstok, Scott L., 1973- author.
Title: How to think like Shakespeare : lessons from a renaissance education /
Scott Newstok.
Description: Princeton : Princeton University Press, [2020] | Includes
bibliographical references and index.
Identifiers: LCCN 2019037256 (print) | LCCN 2019037257 (ebook) |
ISBN 9780691177083 (hardback) | ISBN 9780691201580 (ebook)
Subjects: LCSH: Thought and thinking—Study and teaching. | Shakespeare,
William, 1564-1616. | Rhetoric, Renaissance.
Classification: LCC LB1590.3 .N52 2020 (print) | LCC LB1590.3 (ebook) |
DDC 370.11/2—dc23
LC record available at https://lccn.loc.gov/2019037256
LC ebook record available at https://lccn.loc.gov/2019037257

British Library Cataloging-in-Publication Data is available

Editorial: Anne Savarese and Jenny Tan
Production Editorial: Lauren Lepow
Text and Jacket Design: Lorraine Doneker
Production: Erin Suydam and Danielle Amatucci
Publicity: Jodi Price and Katie Lewis

Jacket image: Shutterstock

This book has been composed in Garamond Premier Pro

Printed on acid-free paper. ∞

Printed in the United States of America

1 3 5 7 9 10 8 6 4 2

Has [he] any brains? . . . Hath he any thinking?
Sure they sleep—he hath no use of them!
—William Shakespeare,
The Merry Wives of Windsor

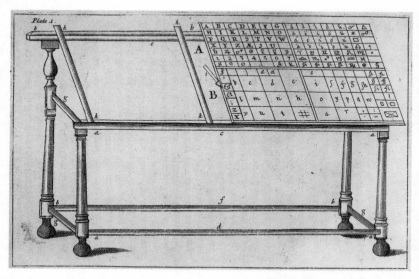

Joseph Moxon, *Mechanick exercises, or, The doctrine of handy-works: applied to the art of printing*, plate 1 (London, 1683). Rare Books and Manuscripts Department, Boston Public Library, G.676 M87R v. 2

CONTENTS

To have consideration for the claims upon your time, I have appended . . . a table of contents of the several books, and have taken very careful precautions to prevent your having to read the books. You by these means will secure for others that they will not need to read right through them either, but only look for the particular point that each of them wants, and will know where to find it.

—Pliny the Elder, *Natural History* (c. 77 CE)

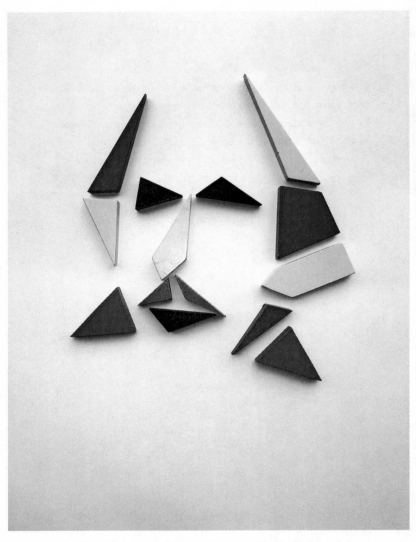

Archimedes's *ostomachion* puzzle, arranged by Ruth Newstok.

WHAT'S PAST IS PROLOGUE

[Shakespeare] almost every where manifests a perfect
knowledge in the anatomy of the human mind.
—Elizabeth Griffith, *The Morality of Shakespeare's
Drama Illustrated* (1775)

In this book of short—deliberately short—chapters, I explore what seem to me to be the key aspects of thinking, and how to hone them. As both a teacher and a parent of school-age children, I've become dismayed by the way we think of thinking. While dismay first animated my writing, I'm hopeful that Shakespearean habits of mind can help us hold a mirror up to current dogma.[1]

Anxiety about education suffuses our moment. What's the purpose of education? Who gets access to it? When and where should it take place? How can we measure it? Will it get us a job? And is it even worth it, when it's both expensive and time-consuming?

Our anxieties derive from many urgent sources, and surge along many rivulets. But underlying them all lies a worrisome muddle about what we even mean by "education."

My conviction is that education must be about *thinking*—not training a set of specific skills.

Education isn't merely accumulating data; machines can memorize far more, and far less fallibly, than humans. (Albert Einstein: *The value of an education . . . is not the learning of many facts but the training of the mind to think something that cannot be learned from textbooks.*)[2]

---

[1] This section's title derives from *The Tempest* (2.1.246)—but reader beware: in its original context, this is an incitement to murder! Unless otherwise noted, all Shakespeare quotations derive from *The Norton Shakespeare*, 3rd ed., edited by Stephen Greenblatt et al. (Norton, 2016).

[2] According to his biographer, this was Einstein's 1921 retort to Thomas Edison mocking

Nor is education merely implementing formulas; machines can execute far more complex algorithms, and at speeds no human can aspire to. (Niels Bohr: *No, no . . . you are not thinking; you are just being logical.*)[3]

Thinking, that elusive yet crucial activity, is different from these. And if humanity has a killer app, this is it. Conversely, the failure to cultivate thinking is a potential killer. Faced with existential crises in the environment, human migration, creeping authoritarianism, and the specter of artificial intelligence, a world without a broadly disseminated capacity for *thinking* is severely exposed.

Who better embodies a fully deployed mind than William Shakespeare, whom we can *almost watch . . . at the task of thinking*?[4] Hence the aim of *How to Think like Shakespeare*. It seeks to offer not only an exploration of thinking, but an enactment of it, for *joy's soul lies in the doing.*[5]

And because the educational assumptions that shaped Shakespeare were at odds with our own, this book explores those assumptions too.

Now, building a bridge to the sixteenth century must seem a perverse prescription for today's ills.[6] If *you* had to be at your desk by 6:00 in the morning, you too would be *creeping like snail / Unwillingly to school*. Raise your hand if you'd like to be beaten for tardiness. What—no takers? OK, how about translating Latin? . . .

---

college as "useless." Philipp Frank, *Einstein: His Life and Times*, trans. George Rosen, ed. Shuichi Kusaka (Knopf, 1947), 185.

   [3] As reported by Otto Robert Frisch, *What Little I Remember* (Cambridge University Press, 1979), 95.

   [4] E. E. Kellett, "Some Notes on a Feature of Shakespeare's Style," in *Suggestions* (Cambridge, 1923), 57–78. I'll confess: I found this quotation in Sister Miriam Joseph's still-wonderful *Shakespeare's Use of the Arts of Language* (1947; Paul Dry Books, 2008), 169. Her study *The Trivium* (1948) remains a gem as well.

   [5] *Troilus and Cressida* (1.3.265).

   [6] I've lifted this phrase from Neil Postman's *Building a Bridge to the Eighteenth Century* (2011). His *Amusing Ourselves to Death* (1985) was the most unsettling book I stumbled upon as a teenager in the Duluth Public Library. Among the many publications with the doomsayer title *The End of Education*, my favorite remains Postman's (1996).

for almost twelve hours a day?... for six days a week?... with no summer vacations? No wonder that when *school broke up* you'd *hurr[y] towards [your] home.*

This education was nasty, brutish, and *long*. Indeed, it was scorned—by Shakespeare himself! Whether it's the huffing Holofernes, the garrulous Gerald, or the schoolmaster Hugh Evans (whose monotone repetition of *William... William* anticipates Ben Stein's *Bueller... Bueller*), Shakespearean teachers come off as *domineering pedants*, overstuffed with *bookish theoric*. Even Prospero faults himself for loving *the liberal arts* so much that he neglected *worldly ends*.[7]

You'd have a hard time designing a system more unlike our own student-centered, present-focused, STEM-driven schools. Moreover, the sixteenth-century exclusion of girls, the poor, and cultural minorities affronts our conviction that *truth must be common to all*.[8] We *do not want art for a few, any more than education for a few, or freedom for a few*.[9]

Just to be clear: I'm not proposing that we reinstate corporal punishment, tedious rote memorization, or schools that exclude anyone. *Thinking is the common property of all*.[10]

Yet it's blinkered to dismiss Shakespeare's instruction as nothing but oppressive. Thinkers trained in this unyielding system went on to generate world-shifting insights, founding forms of knowledge—indeed, the scientific method itself—that continue to shape our lives. An apparently inflexible program of study induced liberated thinking. And we're far from immune from our own inflexible

[7] Whew! that was *a mint of phrases*: *As You Like It* (2.7.144–46); *2 Henry IV* (4.2.271–72); *The Merry Wives of Windsor* (4.1.14–64); *Love's Labor's Lost* (3.1.163); *Othello* (1.1.22); *The Tempest* (1.2.73, 89); *Love's Labor's Lost* (1.1.163).

[8] Mary Wollstonecraft, "Dedication," in *A Vindication of the Rights of Woman* (James Moore, 1793), vi.

[9] William Morris, "The Lesser Arts," in *Hopes and Fears for Art* (1877; Longman, 1930), 35.

[10] Heraclitus, ξυνόν ἐστι πᾶσι τὸ φρονέειν, cited by Haun Saussy, "A Backstage Tour of the Palace of Culture," *History of Humanities* 4, no. 1 (Spring 2019): 62.

idols: our educational system is too often *rigid where it should be yielding, and lax where it should be rigid.*[11]

Thinking like Shakespeare untangles a host of today's confused—let's be blunt: just plain *wrong*[12]—educational binaries. We now act as if work precludes play; imitation impedes creativity; tradition stifles autonomy; constraint limits innovation; discipline somehow contradicts freedom; engagement with what is past and foreign occludes what is present and native.

Shakespeare's era delighted in exposing these purported dilemmas as false: play emerges *through* work, creativity *through* imitation, autonomy *through* tradition, innovation *through* constraints, freedom *through* discipline.[13] I stand with the contrarian view that *to be a political progressive, one needs to be an educational conservative.* Preserving *the seeds of time* enriches the present—call this heirloom education:

> For out of old fields, as people say,
> Comes all this new grain from year to year;
> And out of old books, in good faith,
> Comes all this new knowledge that people learn.[14]

Each of the following fourteen chapters weighs lessons from Shakespeare's world (and work), aligns them with modern-day analogues, and suggests opportunities for further reading. Dis-

---

[11] Alfred North Whitehead sounds as if he could just as easily be writing today as a century ago. *The Aims of Education* (1916; The Free Press, 1967), 13.

[12] As Thomas Paine jabbed in 1776: *a long habit of not thinking a thing wrong, gives it a superficial appearance of being right. Common Sense, and Other Writings,* ed. Gordon Wood (Modern Library, 2003), 5.

[13] Jeanette Winterson goes so far as to say that *no discipline equals no freedom.* "Ten Rules for Writing Fiction (part two)," *Guardian,* February 19, 2010.

[14] Katharine Birbalsingh, Headmistress at Michaela Community College, 2012 Learning Without Frontiers conference, https://www.youtube.com/watch?v=pJx EM_i3iXo. *Macbeth* (1.3.59); Geoffrey Chaucer, *The Parliament of Fowls* (1:22–25), as modernized by Harvard Law School, and a favorite quotation of British jurist Edward Coke.

tilled here are the ingredients of this manner of thinking—a kind of loose recipe for cooking it up.

Because *the investigation of words is the beginning of education*,[15] we'll often pause to ponder the history of a key term, in hopes of amending the impoverished way we've come to talk about one of the richest human endeavors. A more vibrant vocabulary could help make a better *platform of teaching*, to invoke one seventeenth-century educator's evocative phrase.[16] A platform ought to raise us up, not just sell us stuff: *And here I build a platform, and live upon it, and think my thoughts, and aim high.*[17]

Throughout this book, I've stitched together an *almost endless collection of scattered thoughts and observations*[18] into a kind of patchwork, or *cento*, of passages that have inspired me.[19] Be fore-warned: quotations come *"swift as thought," as Homer used to say.*[20] I do this precisely because thinking like Shakespeare means thinking with *each other's / harvest.*[21] And I'm eager for this eclectic chorus of voices to be *the cause that wit is in other[s].*[22]

Little that I say here is new. But if it's true that *there is nothing worth thinking but it has been thought before*, then it's also true that *we must only try to think it again.*[23] And not just think—but restate

[15] Antisthenes, *Artium scriptores*, ed. L. Radermacher, B.19.6.

[16] Charles Hoole, *The Usher's Duty; or, a Platform of Teaching Lily's Grammar* (1637).

[17] Mary Oliver, *Long Life* (Da Capo Press, 2004), 90.

[18] Jean-Jacques Rousseau, *Emile, or On Education* (1762).

[19] Even saying *that* isn't new—just listen to Michel de Montaigne: *I have gathered a posie of other men's flowers, and nothing but the thread that binds them is mine own. Essays of Michel de Montaigne*, "Of Physiognomy," cited by Willis Goth Regier, *Quotology* (University of Nebraska Press, 2010), 107. As Regier notes, John Bartlett liked this quotation so much that he made it the epigraph to the fourth and subsequent editions of his *Familiar Quotations* (Little, Brown and Company, 1863).

[20] Hannah Arendt, "Thinking and Moral Considerations," *Social Research* 38, no. 3 (Autumn 1971): 431.

[21] Gwendolyn Brooks, "Paul Robeson," in *Family Pictures* (Broadside Lotus Press, 1971), 19.

[22] *2 Henry IV* (1.2.9).

[23] Johann Wolfgang von Goethe, *Maxims and Reflections*, trans. Bailey Saunders (Macmillan, 1893), 59.

for our moment: *We have now sunk to a depth at which the restatement of the obvious is the first duty.*[24]

The chapters return to recurrent notions, trusting that *thought does not progress in a single direction; instead, the moments are interwoven as in a carpet.*[25] Anything more direct would betray *our myriad-minded Shakespeare.*[26]

The reason the chapters are no more than fourteen? To paraphrase King Lear: *Because they are not fifteen* (1.5.31). In other words: it's pretty arbitrary!

But in the spirit of the Renaissance fascination with numerical lore, let's play out a few happy congruences (see chapter 4, "Of Fit"). Fortuitously, fourteen aligns with the number of lines in a sonnet (see chapter 12, "Of Constraint"), the stages in the educational *Progymnasmata* (see chapter 9, "Of Exercises"), and the US constitutional amendment guaranteeing citizenship (see chapter 14, "Of Freedom").

Fourteen years is around the age when a student (see chapter 1, "Of Thinking") left grammar school (see chapter 5, "Of Place") after copying good models (8, "Of Imitation") and building up a storehouse of knowledge (11, "Of Stock"). It was the age to enter an apprenticeship (3, "Of Craft") and start a career (13, "Of Making"). For women in particular, the age stood as benchmark for maturity (2, "Of Ends"), as for Juliet, who we're reminded *hath not seen the change of fourteen years,*[27] or in the case of Pericles's fourteen-years-delayed reunion with his daughter Marina (10, "Of Conversation").

The Greek mathematician Archimedes (7, "Of Technology") invented a puzzle called *ostomachion*, which sharpened your mem-

---

[24] George Orwell, in a review of Bertrand Russell's *Power: A New Social Analysis*, in *Adelphi*, January 1939.

[25] Theodor Adorno, "The Essay as Form," in *Notes to Literature* (1958; Columbia University Press, 1991), 13.

[26] Samuel Taylor Coleridge, *Biographia Literaria*, ed. J. Shawcross, 2 vols. (Oxford University Press, 1901), 2:13.

[27] *Romeo and Juliet* (1.2.9).

ory (6, "Of Attention") while you rearranged its fourteen pieces into patterns of *infinite variety*.[28] And many religious traditions find the number significant: Jains believe in fourteen levels of spiritual development; Catholics observe fourteen stations of the Cross; the Passover Seder follows fourteen steps.

More poignantly, the Egyptian god Osiris was said to have been cut into fourteen pieces by his murderous brother Set, who scattered the bits in all directions. John Milton transformed this mythological butchery into a parable about the laborious process of reconstructing thought:

> From that time ever since, the sad friends of Truth, such as durst appear, imitating the careful search that Isis made for the mangled body of Osiris, went up and down gathering up limb by limb, still as they could find them.

Milton concedes: *We have not yet found them all . . . nor ever shall do*.[29]

That's all the more reason to think hard about thinking.

[28] *Antony and Cleopatra* (2.2.248).
[29] *Areopagitica* (1644), in *The Complete Poetry and Essential Prose of John Milton,* ed. William Kerrigan, John Rumrich, and Stephen M. Fallon (Modern Library, 2007), 955.

HOW TO THINK LIKE SHAKESPEARE

The Thinker of Cernavodă. National History Museum of Romania, Bucharest: 15906.
Photo: Marius Amarie.

1
OF THINKING

"I will not cease from mental fight," Blake wrote. Mental
fight means thinking against the current, not with it.
—Virginia Woolf, "Thoughts on Peace
in an Air Raid" (1940)

Thinking's tough. We all want shortcuts; you probably picked up
this book because you thought it would give you shortcuts. Thinking taxes us, because *our brains are designed not for thought but for
the avoidance of thought*.[1] No wonder we dodge it! But don't take
my word for it:

- *Nothing pains some people more than having to think.*
  —Martin Luther King Jr. (1963)

- *Most people would die sooner than think—in fact they do so.*
  —Bertrand Russell (1925)

- *Remember how many pass their whole lives and hardly once think and
  never learned themselves to think.*
  —Walt Whitman (1855)

- *What is the hardest task in the world? To think.*
  —Ralph Waldo Emerson (1841)

- *the very painful Effort of really thinking*
  —Samuel Taylor Coleridge (1811)

[1] Daniel Willingham, *Why Don't Students Like School?* (Jossey-Bass, 2009), 4.

- *A provision of endless apparatus, a bustle of infinite enquiry and research, or even the mere mechanical labour of copying, may be employed, to evade and shuffle off real labour,—the real labour of thinking.*
    —Sir Joshua Reynolds (1784)[2]

Thinking about thinking might be easier to caricature than to capture, whether in iconic images of Rodin's *Thinker* or Hamlet holding Yorick's skull. The novelist William Golding relates how he was chastised as a delinquent student:

> "Don't you ever think at all?"
> No, I didn't think, wasn't thinking, couldn't think—I was simply waiting in anguish for the interview to stop.
> "Then you'd better learn—hadn't you?"
> On one occasion the headmaster leaped to his feet, reached up and plonked Rodin's masterpiece on the desk before me.
> "That's what a man looks like when he's really thinking."
> I surveyed the gentleman without interest or comprehension.[3]

Lewis Carroll mocks the faith that a mere pose will induce insight: when the Dodo can't answer a question

> without a great deal of thought . . . it stood for a long time with one finger pressed upon its forehead (the position in which you usually see Shakespeare, in the pictures of him), while the rest waited in silence.[4]

Even Plato failed to settle upon one apt image for thinking, calling forth, in turn, the sting of a gadfly; the midwifing of a notion; the

[2] King, *Strength to Love* (Harper & Rowe, 1963), 2; Russell, *The ABC of Relativity* (George Allen and Unwin, 1925), 166; Whitman, *Leaves of Grass*, vol. 3, ed. Oscar Lovell Triggs (Putnam's, 1902), 269; Emerson, "The Intellect," in *The Collected Works of Ralph Waldo Emerson*, vol. 2 (Harvard University Press, 1980), 196; Coleridge, *Lectures on Shakespeare (1811–1819)*, ed. Adam Roberts (Edinburgh University Press, 2016), 1:187; Reynolds, *Discourses XII*, in *The Works of Sir Joshua Reynolds*, vol. 1 (1797), 247.
[3] "Party of One: Thinking as a Hobby," *Holiday* 30 (August 1961): 8.
[4] *The Annotated Alice*, ed. Martin Gardner (Norton, 2015), 36.

paralysis induced by an electric ray; an inward conversation; a sudden, invisible wind.

Yet like the famous judge faced with obscenity, we claim to know *thinking* when we see it, despite the difficulty of definition. And if we believe cultivating it is a good thing, then we are often perverse. We've imposed educational programs that kill the capacity to think independently, or even the desire to do so. While we point to thinkers—Leonardo, Galileo, Newton, Darwin, Curie—who model the disciplined, independent, questing intellect we claim to revere, we enforce systems ensuring that our own young people could never emulate them.

Shakespeare earned his place in our pantheon of minds by staging thought in action. Across his works, terms like "think," "thinking," or "thought" outnumber "feel," "feeling," or "felt," by a nearly 10:1 ratio. He raises ideas *into a quasi-physical reality,*[5] vivifying their dynamic power as a palpable force. When staging thinking, Shakespeare adopts images from a craft workshop, whether as thoughts *whirlèd like a potter's wheel,* or *the quick forge and workinghouse of thought*—as if one were *hammer*ing mental metal on an anvil.

He even coins an adjective for thinking, "forgetive." "Forgetive" looks as though it ought to mean something like, well, "*forget*ful." But the emphasis is instead on the kinetic activity in that root "forge": to make or grasp. We must be ready to *fly like thought* to catch it in the act, *for nimble thought can jump both sea and land.*[6] (When Helen Keller placed her hands on Merce Cunningham to feel him leap, she marveled: *How like thought. How like the mind it is.*)[7]

As Shakespeare's contemporary Michel de Montaigne put it,

---

[5] Ted Hughes, *Shakespeare and the Goddess of Complete Being* (Faber and Faber, 1992), 153.

[6] *1 Henry VI* (1.6.19); *Henry V* (5.0.23); *Richard II* (5.5.5); *2 Henry IV* (4.2.91); *King John* (4.2.175); sonnet 44, line 7.

[7] As recounted in Martha Graham's memoir *Blood Memory* (Doubleday, 1991), 98.

thinking about thinking is *a thorny undertaking, and more so than it seems, to follow a movement so wandering as that of our mind.*[8]

Here's a recent example of *not* thinking about Shakespearean thinking.

Ken Robinson's "Do Schools Kill Creativity?" is a popular TED talk, with more than sixty million views. The title primes your answer: *yes—yes, of course schools kill creativity.* And Robinson's pitch follows his self-confirming template:

> schools are _____ [hierarchical/industrialist/outdated];
> this is a _____ [crisis/crime/catastrophe];
> and the answer is _____ [creativity/innovation/technology].

Yet his diagnoses and his prescriptions don't line up, right from his disarming opening joke:

> . . . you don't think of Shakespeare being a child, do you?
> Shakespeare being seven?
> I never thought of it.
> I mean, he was seven at some point.
> He was in somebody's English class, wasn't he?
> How annoying would that be?
> *"Must try harder."*

Sir Ken gets the laughs. But Shakespeare never studied in an "English class"; no such class would exist until centuries after his time. Instead, his Stratford grammar school was conducted in Latin. And his regimented Latin curriculum proved to be the crucible for his creative achievement—in English.

Robinson is right about one thing: Shakespeare would have been enrolled at around the age of seven—long considered a pivotal developmental stage for children, as lasting patterns of thinking take hold. Aristotle held that children should leave home and enter school when they turned seven. At seven, medieval pages

---

[8] "Of Practice," in *The Complete Essays of Montaigne*, trans. Donald Frame (Stanford University Press, 1958), 273.

would enter the household of a knight. It's the age that Michael Apted's *Seven Up* documentary commences its remarkable chronicle of the life-determining effects of social class, summoning the motto attributed to Loyola: *Give me the child for the first seven years, and I will give you the man.*

In 2016, I was invited to address my college's incoming students. My summer was consumed with fretting that the last thing they'd want to hear would be a lecture from some forty-three-year-old white man.

Indeed, my microdemographic had just become a reverse meme! An irritated millennial journalist had replaced the word "millennials" in magazine headlines with the phrase "43-Year-Old White Men,"[9] exposing fatuous generational generalizations:

"How 43-Year-Old White Men Are Ruining the Workforce"
"Why Are So Many 43-Year-Old White Men Having Zero Sex?"
"The Hot New 43-Year-Old White Men Trend Is Hating 43-Year-Old White Men"

and my favorite:

"Martha Stewart Still Confused about What 43-Year-Old White Men Are Exactly"

So I was cautious about being the cranky old prof hectoring the youth.

But it dawned on me: *these students would have been seven years old* just around the moment that our obsession with shallow forms of evaluation was kicking into high gear. Their cohort was the first to have been marched through their entire primary and secondary schooling under a testing-obsessed regime. (While I concentrate here on the American system, this is a global phenomenon, as fellow teachers from South Korea to Kurdistan have recounted to me.)

---

[9] Amanda Rosenberg, "I Replaced the Word 'Millennials' with '43-Year-Old White Men' and Now These Headlines Are *Italian Chef Kissing Fingers Gesture,*" *SlackJaw*, August 24, 2016.

In December 2001, just as I was stumbling to the close of my first semester of full-time teaching, the No Child Left Behind Act passed Congress with support from both parties as well as educational entrepreneurs—yet with scant input from actual *teachers*. We were promised the act would close the achievement gap, to make all students proficient in reading and math by the year 2014. Perversely, its so-called "skills"-driven focus on literacy and numeracy did *not* lead to greater literacy and numeracy. Instead, the achievement gap widened, as draconian reforms sapped scarce time and resources from course offerings in art, drama, music, history, languages, and even the sciences.

Teachers' autonomy was eroded by external curricular mandates, often directed by corporate vendors eager to advance Bill Gates's vision of standardizing education as if it were *an electrical plug* or *railroad width* [*sic!*].[10] This disempowerment of teachers makes them little more than paraprofessionals. They're present not to model thinking, just to help the machines hoover up a child's "data exhaust" and monitor *learnification*.[11]

Yet the wealthier you are, the more likely you will be to insist that *your* child's school, nanny, and other caretakers *not* expose them to attention-splintering digital fora. John Dewey's exhortation still ought to ring true:

> What the best and wisest parent wants for his own child, that must the community want for all of its children. Any other ideal for our schools is narrow and unlovely; acted upon, it destroys our democracy.[12]

Worse, high-stakes exams narrowed not only *what's* taught, but *how* it's taught. The open-ended joy of reading has too often withered to a soulless dissection of *content* without *context*; the joy of

[10] See Stephanie Simon, "Bill Gates Plugs Common Core," *Politico*, September 24, 2014. *Sic* is the Latin for "thus," as in "Yeah, I can't believe he actually said that, but he really did." But I also like that it's pronounced the same as *sick*!

[11] Gert Biesta's caustic term for the attack on teachers' active role in our classrooms.

[12] *The School and Society* (University of Chicago Press, 1900), 19.

mathematics to arbitrary exercises, drained of the delightful pattern making that generates conjecture in the first place.[13] We've forgotten Mark Twain's insight: *Intellectual "work" is misnamed; it is a pleasure, a dissipation, and is its own highest reward.*[14]

I was a math geek before I finally determined to study literature. I'll never forget how my college calculus professor, renowned for his intimidating personality, would stop in the midst of a proof. He'd step back from the chalkboard. He'd stare, and ponder: "Look at that. Do you see that? We could have done this proof in eleven steps, but we found a more elegant way—we got there in just seven. That's . . . that's *beautiful.*" His awe at the grace-filled solution was contagious: *A mathematician, like a painter or a poet, is a maker of patterns.*[15]

All intellectual pursuits are more *qualitative* than any bubble sheet can ever gauge. We ought not to be surprised that in recent decades children have become

> less emotionally expressive, less energetic, less talkative and verbally expressive, less humorous, less imaginative, less unconventional, less lively and passionate, less perceptive, less apt to connect seemingly irrelevant things, less synthesizing, and less likely to see things from a different angle.[16]

This is the real creativity-killer.

Let's return now to seven-year-old Shakespeare, and consider not "how annoying" he might have been to his instructor, but

---

[13] I commend Paul Lockhart's "A Mathematician's Lament" (2009): https://www.maa.org/external_archive/devlin/LockhartsLament.pdf.

[14] *A Connecticut Yankee in King Arthur's Court* (1889), ed. Bernard L. Stein (University of California Press, 2010), 279.

[15] British mathematician G. H. Hardy, cited in Karen Olsson, "The Aesthetic Beauty of Math," *Paris Review* blog, July 22, 2019: https://www.theparisreview.org/blog/2019/07/22/the-aesthetic-beauty-of-math/.

[16] Kyung-Hee Kim, summarizing the data from the 2011 Torrance Tests of Creative Thinking, cited in Peter Gray, "The Play Deficit," *Aeon*, September 18, 2013. Writing *is not a matter of filling in blanks in workbooks, but rather a joyful form of expression.* Helen Vendler, "Reading Is Elemental," *Harvard Magazine*, September, 2011.

rather how we might reclaim some of the best aspects of his education.

Now, I know what you're thinking: *of course* a Shakespeare professor would say that—we all tend to think the thing that *we* do is right, as in Alexander Pope's observation:

'Tis with our judgments as our watches, none
Go just alike, yet each believes his own.[17]

Shakespeare's contemporary Philip Sidney jested that all people praise their own line of work as essential. Before he defends his own hobbyhorse (poetry), Sidney recounts another man's affection for horsemanship:

He exercised his speech in the praise of his faculty. He said soldiers were the noblest estate of mankind, and horsemen the noblest of soldiers . . . [and that] no earthly thing bred such wonder to a prince as to be a good horseman. . . . [he nearly] persuaded me to have wished myself a horse.[18]

I don't wish you were a horse! or even another Shakespeare, who *will never be made by the study of Shakespeare*.[19]

Yet Shakespeare was once seven; he did have teachers; and they taught him something about thinking. In turn, our own power of understanding can *expand and become conscious of itself as we watch it at work in Shakespeare*.[20]

I'm not talking about *what* Shakespeare thought. Every word onstage is said through the voice of a character, so wrenching quotations out of context won't reveal how he felt about law or love or leadership. This hasn't prevented management consultants from

---

[17] *An Essay on Criticism* (1709), lines 9–10.
[18] *The Defense of Poesy* (1595), in *Selected Writings*, ed. Richard Dutton (Routledge, 2002), 102.
[19] Ralph Waldo Emerson, "Self-Reliance" (1841), in *The Prose Works of Ralph Waldo Emerson*, vol. 1 (1870), 259.
[20] John Middleton Murry, "The Process of Creative Style," in *The Problem of Style* (Oxford University Press, 1922), 116.

claiming that they can derive lessons from the plays. Here's a familiar example:

> This above all: to thine own self be true,
> And it must follow as the night the day
> Thou canst not then be false to any man.[21]

One book glosses these lines thus: *Trust and integrity are critical in business. . . . once one's reputation for integrity is lost, one's effectiveness is lost.*[22]

The blandness is obvious. And I have to confess: I'm guilty of this kind of misguided projection. My high school yearbook from three decades ago includes my pimpled portrait, nerdy activities, and classmates' scribbles. For my motto, I selected this same passage from *Hamlet*. And I attributed those words to . . . "Shakespeare."

But the quotation comes from a sententious father reciting a cascade of tepid proverbs to his departing son. So *what* "Shakespeare said" (here, a trite truism) is far less suggestive than *how* it was said (through the voice of a toadying functionary). This character satirizes moral entrepreneurship![23]

Look at the peculiar way this speech was first printed in 1603. Why does the left margin insert a series of quotation marks? The punctuation flags you to *stop, look, notice* these sententious phrases; *transcribe* them in your commonplace book. Here you might jot down new words, favorite phrases, ideas caught in passing. Anything that *your memory cannot contain / Commit to these waste blanks* (sonnet 77).

Thomas Hobbes always carried *a Note-book in his pocket, and as soon as a notion darted, he presently entered it into his Booke, or els*

---

[21] *Hamlet* (1.3.77–79).
[22] Jay M. Shafritz, *Shakespeare on Management* (Carol Publishing, 1992), 95.
[23] Jeffrey R. Wilson, "What Shakespeare Says about Sending Our Children Off to College," *Academe* 102, no. 3 (May/June 2016).

The winde fits in the fhoulder of your faile,
And you are ftaid for, there my bleffing with thee
And thefe few precepts in thy memory.
" Be thou familiar, but by no meanes vulgare;
" Thofe friends thou haft, and their adoptions tried,
'• Graple them to thee with a hoope of fteele,
" But do not dull the palme with entertaine,
" Of euery new vnfleg'd courage,
" Beware of entrance into a quarrell;but being in,
" Beare it that the oppofed may beware of thee,
" Coftly thy apparrell, as thy purfe can buy.
" But not expreft in fafhion,
" For the apparell oft proclaimes the man.
And they of *France* of the chiefe rancke and ftation
Are of a moft felect and generall chiefe in that:
" This aboue all, to thy owne felfe be true,
And it muft follow as the night the day,

Page from *Hamlet* (1603). Courtesy of Henry E. Huntington Library. Rare Book number 69304.

he should perhaps have lost it.[24] In such a notebook, an aspiring young thinker archives choice thoughts for later reflection, and eventual action.[25] According to one Renaissance treatise,

> it is singular good, to have some pretie sprinckled judgement in the common places and practizes of all the liberall sciences, chopt up in hotchpot togither, out of the whiche we may still help ourselves in talke.[26]

By compiling commonplace thoughts of others, we can better shape our own words to become, well, less commonplace.

Books about what Shakespeare "thought" about love also strip

[24] John Aubrey, *Aubrey's Brief Lives*, ed. Oliver Lawson Dick (David Godine, 1999), 351.

[25] Augustine: *discitur ut agatur*—"it is learned, so that it may be done," *On Christian Doctrine* (4.13.29).

[26] Philibert de Viennne, *The Philosopher of the Court* (1547), translated by George North (1575).

quotations of their situational meaning. Sonnets are often contorted to fit sexual conventions. You might hear sonnet 18 or 116 recited at a wedding between a man and a woman:

> Shall I compare thee to a summer's day?
> Thou art more lovely and more temperate.

Or

> Let me not to the marriage of true minds
> Admit impediments. Love is not love
> Which alters when it alteration finds.

Yet they're in the voice of an older man addressing his younger male intimate. And once again, the *how*—sonnet 18's jaunty query, or sonnet 116's defiant negations (*not . . . not*)—is far more intriguing here than the *what* of the love lyric, which often amounts to little more than *I need you, you need me, yum, yum.*[27]

I'm suggesting that *to think like Shakespeare*, we need to reconsider the habits that shaped his mind, including practices as simple as transcribing quotations, or working with a tradition. Doing these things doesn't mean that you will become "the next Shakespeare"; neither you nor I have the same alchemy of talents and circumstances as anyone else. And as Desiderius Erasmus insisted: even Cicero wouldn't write like Cicero if he were alive today.[28]

But Shakespearean thinking does demand a deliberate engagement with the past to help you make up your mind in the present. In the words of Ralph Ellison: *Some people are your relatives but others are your ancestors, and you choose the ones you want to have as ancestors. You create yourself out of those values.*[29]

---

[27] Frank O'Hara, "Blocks," cited by Helen Vendler in *The Art of Shakespeare's Sonnets* (Harvard University Press, 1997), 14.

[28] *we speak fittingly only when our speech is consistent with the persons and conditions of present day life.*
Ciceronianus, or, A Dialogue on the Best Style of Speaking (1528), trans. Izora Scott (Teachers College, 1908), 61. As Emrys Jones puts it: *without Erasmus, no Shakespeare. The Origins of Shakespeare* (Oxford University Press, 1977), 13.

[29] *Time* 83, no. 13 (March 27, 1964): 67.

William Blake, Illustration 7 to Milton's *Paradise Lost*: The Rout of the Rebel Angels (1807). Courtesy of the Huntington Art Collections, San Marino, California. Object Number: 000.8.

2
OF ENDS

setting down their journey's end ere they attain to it
they rest, and travel not so far as they should
—Francis Bacon, to the Earl of Rutland (1596)

What is the end of study? the sardonic character Biron jests in *Love's Labor's Lost* (1.1.55). He's balking at the strict terms of a mutual oath: study relentlessly, sleep little, diet austerely, avoid the company of women. As the play will prove, the end of study is not love; it's not philosophy; it's not erudition; it's not showy language; it's not subservience to the past; it's not a fixation on present fashions.

So the question lingers: *What is the end of study?* Why learn?

Faustus's first speech similarly challenges educational orthodoxy, seeking to *settle thy studies . . . level at the end of every art,* as if he were a sophomore, pondering potential careers. After dismissing logic and medicine as professions he's already mastered, he dispenses with law and divinity too. Necromancy it is! He signs his blasphemous contract with the devil: *Consummatum est; this bill is ended.*[1]

Faustus and Biron both chafe at the consensus surrounding the end of study. While I trust you haven't signed anything in blood lately, I do worry that we've made our own kind of Faustian bargain with education. Because we've given up on any collective *end,* we resort to inoffensive nostrums like *the aim of education is to enable individuals to continue their education.*[2]

---

[1] Christopher Marlowe, *Doctor Faustus* (1.1.1–4, 2.1.74). *Doctor Faustus: A- And B-Texts,* ed. David Bevington and Eric Rasmussen (Manchester University Press, 1993).

[2] John Dewey, *Democracy and Education* (Macmillan, 1916), 117.

Is this the phrase that launched a thousand mission statements?

As we hear in both Biron and Faustus, "end" can indicate a "goal" or "culmination," as in the Latin *finis*; "end" can resonate with a philosophical sense of "purpose" or "function," as in the Greek *telos*; and "end" can conjure up more ominous undertones of violence, as in *The Comedy of Errors* (4.4.15–17).

"The end of " might well be the *perfect headline for our age*, as it *fits a moment that fetishizes disruption over stability*.[3] "The End of Study" or "The End of School" or "The End of Education" are hyperventilated phrases that have been marshaled *against* teachers at all levels. Advocates of educational technology are prone to apocalyptic overtones, contemptuous of conventional classroom instruction. For champions of so-called disruptive innovation, it would be a *good* thing if half of US universities went bankrupt, and *by the year 2019 half of all classes for grades K–12 [were] taught online*.[4]

But the ed-tech-industrial complex's fetishizing of *means* is symptomatic of our deeper ailment, the *inner contradiction of an end that is the endless production of means without an end*.[5] Already by the late nineteenth century, Friedrich Nietzsche felt that education had

> lost sight of the most important thing: the *end* as well as the *means* to the end. That schooling, *education* is an end in itself.... our 'high' schools are without exception geared to the most ambiguous mediocrity, with teachers, teaching plans, teaching objectives.[6]

Nietzsche would have found grimly familiar Nicholson Baker's recent stint as a substitute teacher, where his primary task seemed to be little more than handing out worksheets:

[3] Carlos Lozada, "The End of Everything," *Washington Post*, April 5, 2013.

[4] Courtney Boyd Myers, citing Harvard Business School's Clayton Christensen, "Why Online Education Is Ready for Disruption, Now," *The Next Web*, November 13, 2011.

[5] Paul Tillich, *The Spiritual Situation in Our Technical Society* (Mercer University Press, 1988), 80.

[6] *Twilight of the Idols: or, How to Philosophize with a Hammer* (1889), trans. Duncan Large (Oxford University Press, 1998), 40.

Every high-school subject, no matter how worthy and jazzy and thought-provoking it may have seemed to an earnest Common Corer, is stuffed into the curricular Veg-O-Matic, and out comes a nasty packet with grading rubrics on the back. On the first page, usually, there are numbered "learning targets," and inside, inevitably, a list of specialized vocabulary words to master. . . . This is all fluff knowledge, meta-knowledge.[7]

The reflexive call for educational "targets" in current jargon makes me feel as if we adults have become like William Tell, cruelly aiming arrows at our own children. Our means (passing the test) have overtaken our ends (human flourishing). And if you talk to any archer, you'll discover that to hit a target, *aiming is way overrated.*[8]

So what's a better focus than aiming at the target? According to the counterintuitive advice of the coach just quoted, *Three things: Form, form, and form. If you shoot good form, aiming takes care of itself. It is a self-correcting process.*

Chuang Tzu (Zhuangzi) captured the distorting effect of high-stakes competition:

When an archer is shooting for nothing
He has all his skill.
If he shoots for a brass buckle
He is already nervous.
If he shoots for a prize of gold
He goes blind
Or sees two targets—
He is out of his mind!

His skill has not changed. But the prize
Divides him. He cares.

---

[7] "Fortress of Tedium: What I Learned as a Substitute Teacher," *New York Times*, September 7, 2016.

[8] Terry Wunderle, cited by Bill Heavey, "How to Put an Arrow in Your Target Every Time," *Field and Stream*, August 31, 2005.

> He thinks more of winning
> Than of shooting—
> And the need to win
> Drains him of power.[9]

The prize divides him—I'll bet we've all experienced some version
of this. In my final high school track race, my shoulders tensed up
so much in the last stretch that I could scarcely cross the finish line.
I was living Zeno's paradox!

If you create an incentive to hit the target, it's all the *less* likely
that you will be able to do so. The best way to pass a test is . . . by
not fixating on the test. Instead, you must find ways to become
immersed in activity for its own sake, in the company of skilled
practitioners. In his treatise on archery, Elizabethan schoolmaster
Roger Ascham lamented the decline in shooting skills due to *blind
use*—that is, practice without the expert guidance of knowledge-
able instructors, leading to *much illfavoredness and deformity*.[10] In
the words of Rabbi Heschel, *What we need more than anything else
is not text-books but text-people.*[11]

Aiming beyond the short-term target is proverbial wisdom,
from George Herbert (*who aimeth at the sky, / Shoots higher much,
than he that means a tree*) to Henry Wadsworth Longfellow (*If you
would hit the mark, you must aim a little above it*) to Paul Klee (*Be
winged arrows, aiming at fulfillment and goal, even though you will
tire without having reached the mark*).[12]

Niccolò Machiavelli urged us to "aim high" in our selection of
intellectual role models, so that we *behave like those archers who* . . .

---

[9] "The Need to Win," translated by Thomas Merton, from *The Collected Poems of Thomas Merton*, copyright ©1977 by The Trustees of the Merton Legacy Trust. Reprinted by permission of New Directions Publishing Corp.

[10] *Toxophilus* (1545), which means *lover of the bow*.

[11] Abraham Joshua Heschel, "The Spirit of Jewish Education," *Jewish Education* 24, no. 2 (Fall 1953): 19.

[12] *The Church Porch* (56.3–4); "Elegiac Verse" XI, in *The Poetical Works of Henry Wadsworth Longfellow* (Houghton Mifflin, 1885), 297; *Pedagogical Sketchbook*, trans. Sibyl Moholy-Nagy (Faber and Faber, 1984), 54.

aim a good deal higher than their objective, not in order to shoot so high but so that by aiming high they can reach the target.[13] I'm not against testing as a way for teachers to gauge progress within the domain of their own classrooms. But our fixation on test as target, as the *end* of education itself—that shoots an arrow right through the heart of thinking, for *when a measure becomes a target, it ceases to be a good measure.*[14]

I teach in Memphis, the bull's-eye of assessment-driven reforms.[15] No other school district in the nation received funding from both the Gates Foundation and Race to the Top. Onerous evaluation systems proliferated, with predictable results: *new state policies put everyone under stress, are divisive, and suck the joy out of a building.*[16]

Once, when I was volunteering as a literacy tutor in my elder daughter's elementary school, I heard yet another announcement about yet another test preparation strategy barked yet again over the public-address system. I've forgotten the arbitrary acrostic . . . it was something like

Always remember to READ!

REVIEW your question;

EVALUATE its terms;

ASSESS your process;

and

DOUBLE-CHECK your answer—

READ!

I turned to the teacher, a reticent woman who had shielded her students from as much of this nonsense as she could. We had never

---

[13] *The Prince* (1532), trans. George Bull (Penguin, 2003), 19.

[14] Marilyn Strathern's rephrasing of what's known as "Goodhart's Law," named after the chief economic adviser to the Bank of England in the 1970s. "Improving Ratings: Audit in the British University System," *European Review* 5, no. 3 (1997): 305–21.

[15] See Mary Cashiola, "Memphis as a Model" *Memphis Flyer*, July 15, 2010; David Waters, "Costly Failures Come with Lesson," *Daily Memphian*, May 8, 2019.

[16] Michael Winerip, citing Will Shelton, principal of Blackman Middle School. "In Tennessee, Following the Rules for Evaluations Off a Cliff," *New York Times*, November 6, 2011.

spoken more than a few words before. But in my bafflement, I couldn't help but ask her what she thought about this unceasing focus on test preparation. She confided: *I think it's cruelty to children.*

A few days later, my wife and I had a spirit-crushing exchange when we asked our seven-year-old whether she had learned any new words that month. This otherwise vivacious child contemplated a moment, looked at us coldly, and whispered: *assessment.* We had to laugh in bitter recognition; she was right, we'd never uttered that word in our home.

Assessment has become costly, in terms of both time and money. Cumulative *months* of instructional hours are devoted to little more than soul-grinding test preparation.[17] Although *assessors have known for some time now that assessment does not work,*[18] they keep calling for more of it,[18] as if they were heeding Bassanio's advice about how to find a lost arrow: *To shoot another arrow that self [same] way / Which you did shoot the first.*[19]

More of the same—*trying to do the wrong things righter*[20]—will only exacerbate problems of cost, morale, and perverse incentives.

Some educators have even contorted etymology in service of assessment, claiming that the Latin root *assidere* means *sit beside,* in a benign sense—likening it to a teacher, sitting beside a student. Would that it were so! But this has nothing to do with the word's history, which derives from the assessment of property value, for the levying of taxes.

---

[17] It's estimated that *teachers lose between 60 to 110 hours of instructional time in a year because of testing and the institutional tasks that surround it.* National Council of Teachers of English, "How Standardized Tests Shape—and Limit—Student Learning" (2014): http://www.ncte.org/library/NCTEFiles/Resources/Journals/CC/0242-nov2014/CC0242PolicyStandardized.pdf.

[18] Erik Gilbert, "An Insider's Take on Assessment: It May Be Worse Than You Thought," *Chronicle of Higher Education,* January 12, 2018. See his blog, *Bad Assessment*: http://badassessment.org. The 2013 Gordon Commission report draws the same self-serving conclusion: assessment doesn't work, so we need more of it!

[19] *The Merchant of Venice* (1.1.148–49).

[20] Management theorist Russell Ackoff, paraphrasing Peter Drucker. Interviewed by Phyllis Haynes (2001): https://youtu.be/MzS5V5-0VsA.

In Shakespeare's time, an assessor would travel an annual circuit, and would *sit beside* you to estimate the amount you owed in taxes to the government. The assessor is an evaluator who comes close, but only temporarily, in order to surveil you, and to extract value from you on behalf of a distant authority.

It's a cliché, but assessment takes the sterile path of least resistance and crowds out all else. Rather than measure what matters, assessment measures what's easy to measure.[21] Think of Hamlet, lamenting the meaninglessness of even hyperbolic numbers when we are dealing with the unquantifiable:

> I loved Ophelia. Forty thousand brothers
> Could not with all their quantity of love
> Make up my sum. (5.1.248–50)

Quantification has its utility, but we must keep reminding ourselves of how *limited* that utility is. There are spheres where quantity is ineffective in gauging *quality*—indeed, most of the spheres that matter!—like life, love, and learning.

And yet administrators continue to recite the mantra, attributed to Edwards Deming, *If you can't measure it, you can't manage it*. A board member once intoned this line when I maintained that what unfolds in a classroom involves something more *rich and strange*[22] than mere numerical evaluations could ever measure.

In fairness, Deming ought to get partial credit, because it's only part of his quotation. What he said was . . . the opposite: *It is wrong to suppose that if you can't measure it, you can't manage it—a costly myth.*[23]

I'm reminded of the gruesome Grimm version of "Cinderella":

---

[21] Stefan Collini has documented the woeful reign of *impact*, *assessment*'s hydra-headed cousin in the United Kingdom, in *Speaking of Universities* (Verso, 2017). The toxic impact of "impact" in scientific studies has been exposed by Mario Biagioli, in *Nature*: http://www .nature.com/news/watch-out-for-cheats-in-citation-game-1.20246. As I warn my students, if your school says your education has *impacted* you, ask for a refund—and a laxative.

[22] *The Tempest* (1.2.400).

[23] *The New Economics for Industry, Government, Education* (Massachusetts Institute of Technology, Center for Advanced Educational Services, 1993), 36.

if the shoe doesn't fit, chop off toes until it does. People want to take this dictum as doxa, even though mounting evidence confirms that a fixation upon assessment perverts process. *Give a small boy a hammer, and he will find that everything he encounters needs pounding.*[24]

Assessment is the hammer pounding education, turning us into the tools John Ruskin warned us against:

> You must either make a tool of the creature, or a man of him. You cannot make both. Men are not intended to work with the accuracy of tools, to be precise and perfect in all their actions. If you will have that precision out of them, and make their fingers measure degrees like cogwheels, and their arms strike curves like compasses, you must unhumanize them.[25]

Assessment is all about being a cog in the machine. But this machine is pushing us toward various disasters. Education needs to give people the capacity and the confidence to challenge the machine. We need a counternarrative to the merciless logic of drilling, breaking down all knowledge into the smallest assessable unit, what Nietzsche scorned as *an enormous heap of indigestible knowledge-stones.*[26]

Thomas Gradgrind is the model for this kind of administrator, determined to fill "the little pitchers before him . . . full of facts." In Charles Dickens's 1854 novel *Hard Times*, "Murdering the Innocents" is the unsubtle title for the chapter that depicts Gradgrind's persona as *a kind of cannon loaded to the muzzle with facts, and prepared to blow them clean out of the regions of childhood at one discharge.*[27]

We've discharged a sense of the *end*. As W.E.B. Du Bois chal-

[24] Abraham Kaplan's "Law of the Instrument," in *The Conduct of Inquiry* (Chandler, 1964), 28.

[25] *The Stones of Venice* (Smith, Elder, and Co., 1851), 2:162.

[26] *The Complete Works of Friedrich Nietzsche: The First Complete and Authorised English Translation*, vol. 5 (Gordon Press, 1974), 31.

[27] James L. Hughes, *Dickens as an Educator* (University Press of the Pacific, 2001), 121.

lenged us: Is the end of study *to earn meat*? or *to know the end and aim of that life which meat nourishes*?[28] I'm worried we've tilted too much toward the utilitarian end—study as the means to other ends, not for the enlargement of human capacities. The spirit of the times seems instead to be caught up in a *joyless urgency, many of us preparing ourselves and our children to be means to inscrutable ends that are utterly not our own.*[29]

Abraham Flexner, the reformer of medical education, was adamant about the *usefulness of useless knowledge*. According to Flexner, *the really great discoveries* have *been made by men and women who were driven not by the desire to be useful but merely the desire to satisfy their curiosity.*[30] He chronicled scientists like Paul Ehrlich, whose work *just fooling around* in the laboratory led to a remedy for syphilis. Apple Computer was cofounded by someone who insisted that the most vital topic he ever studied was not engineering but . . . *calligraphy*. In other words, he learned enduring principles of precision, beauty, and design. When Shakespeare was born, there wasn't yet a professional theater in London. His "useless" Latin drills prepared him for a job that didn't yet exist. (Who says rhyme doesn't pay!) Why are *we* wasting precious classroom hours on fleeting technical skills—skills that will become obsolete before graduates enter the workforce?

Even though the argument for deferred utility happens to be valid, it hasn't persuaded skeptical funders or legislators. It concedes too much to the lexicon of "use"—and *what is the use of use?*[31] Thorstein Veblen insisted that asking, *What is the use of this learning?* is as ludicrous as Lewis Carroll's Walrus asking *why the sea is boiling hot, / And whether pigs have wings.*[32] Even the

---

[28] *The Souls of Black Folk* (1903; Penguin, 1996), 69.

[29] Marilynne Robinson, "Humanism, Science, and the Radical Expansion of the Possible," *Nation*, October 22, 2015.

[30] *The Usefulness of Useless Knowledge* (1939; Princeton University Press, 2017), 56.

[31] Gotthold Ephraim Lessing, as cited by Hannah Arendt, *Between Past and Future* (Penguin, 2006), 80.

[32] *The Higher Learning in America: A Memorandum on the Conduct of Universities by Business Men* (B. W. Huebsch, 1918), 210.

pragmatic Benjamin Franklin once retorted to such a query: *What's the use of a baby?*[33] Shakespeare's plaintive cry in sonnet 65 comes to mind: *How with this rage shall beauty hold a plea, / Whose action is no stronger than a flower?*

We know education has to be useful, to have utility. The problem is that in general and popular usage, "utility" has come to have a truncated sense; even we teachers have acquiesced in this diminished meaning: only that which provides quick and direct returns. The speed with which a student gets a first job, the entry-level pay; the quarterly, at best yearly, return on investment. "Utility tools"; "utilities," light, gas, and water.

We've lost the modifiers: *material* utility, *short-term* utility. Our inability to engage with the whole spectrum of "utility" harms us all, in the end. We have to demand of ourselves that we invoke the fuller phrasing in order to force ourselves to perceive the bias, and thereby accord value more proportionately. Long-term utility cannot come from fixating upon short-term utility.

For Aristotle, the end of study (long-term utility) was to develop citizens who would flourish in a democracy.[34] Education cultivated habits for the end of becoming *a good [person], skilled in speaking,*[35] with an eye toward action: *To be a speaker of words and a doer of deeds.*[36]

The vast apparatus of the curriculum that evolved over the next two millennia sought what Sidney called *the highest end* of self-knowledge: *the end of well-doing, and not of well-knowing only.*[37]

[33] I. Bernard Cohen, *Benjamin Franklin's Science* (Harvard University Press, 1996), 264n11.

[34] See especially *Politics*, bks. 7 and 8.

[35] Cato the Elder's definition of an orator, cited as indisputable truth: *Orator est . . . vir bonus dicendi peritus.* Fragment 14 of a letter to his son. Seneca includes it in his *Controversiae*, as does Quintilian in his *Institutes* (10.1.1).

[36] Homer, *Iliad* (9.455), translated by Stanley Lombardo (Hackett, 1997), 58.

[37] *The Defense of Poesy* (1595), in *Selected Writings*, ed. Richard Dutton (Routledge, 2002), 128. See also the motto from Geoffrey Whitney's *Choice of Emblemes* (1586): *usus libri non lectio prudentes facit.*
Roughly: "the *use* of a book, not just *reading* it, makes us wise."

All the end of study, as John Adams enjoined his son John Quincy, is to make *a useful citizen*.[38]

The method for training this complete citizen was *rhetoric*—a term that we now either consign to tedious catalogs of literary terms or, worse, identify with empty promises, things politicians *say* but don't *mean*. But in Shakespeare's era, rhetoric was nothing less than the fabric of thought itself. Rhetoric wasn't just part of the curriculum; it *was* the curriculum. Because thinking and speaking well form the basis of existence in a community, rhetoric prepares you for any occasion that requires words—it's the craft of future discourse.[39]

That's why students devoted endless hours to its full arsenal of strategies for encompassing a situation: imitating vivid models, exercising elaborate verbal patterning, practicing imaginative writing, and building up an enormous inventory of reading. Fierce attention to clear and precise writing is the essential tool to foster independent judgment; indeed, *precision of thought is essential to every aspect and walk of life*.[40] *That* is rhetoric.

In the absence of an end, means overtake ends. To cite Biron, again:

> So study evermore is overshot.
> While it doth study to have what it would,
> It doth forget to do the thing it should;
> And when it hath the thing it hunteth most,
> 'Tis won as towns with fire: so won, so lost.[41]

Shortsighted educational targets might be the self-destructive end—as in death—of study: hence it may *forget to do the thing it should*.

[38] May 18, 1781: https://founders.archives.gov/documents/Adams/04-04-02-0082.

[39] *future discourse* was a favorite notion of rhetoric historian James J. Murphy throughout his career.

[40] Antoine Arnauld, *The Art of Thinking* (1662), trans. James Dickoff and Patricia James (Library of Liberal Arts, 1964), 7.

[41] *Love's Labor's Lost* (1.1.140–44).

Lekythos, c. 550–530 BCE (terracotta), Amasis Painter (fl. c. 560–515 BCE). Image copyright © The Metropolitan Museum of Art. Image source: Art Resource, NY.

3
OF CRAFT

You can learn how to use your mind in the act of
handling parts and working. You learn how to
work. You learn how things go together.
—Gary Snyder, "The Real Work" (1977)

"Assessment," "targets," "rubrics," "learning outcomes," and the like
all call to mind what E. M. Forster quipped about spoon-feeding:
In the long run [it] teaches us nothing but the shape of the spoon.[1]

What's a better way to talk about vibrant habits of mind? I
propose that *craft* more accurately describes (and celebrates) thinking, whether in Shakespeare's era or ours. *Craft* reminds us of the
writer-in-process that Shakespeare was—a product of his practice,
just as we can be.

I first appreciated the demanding scope of *craft* as a graduate
student, when I lived in a cooperative house. Among the detritus
from former co-op residents: a forlorn upright piano. It wasn't just
out of tune—it was unplayable. Ivory tops were missing. Half the
keys made no noise whatsoever, no matter how hard you hit them.
Eager to get the piano functioning again, I called every tuner in
the Boston Yellow Pages. (Yes, this was the 1990s.) Each time I
described our paltry budget and the piano's state of disrepair, the
tuner I was speaking with declined.

---

[1] September 29, 1951. *The BBC Talks of E. M. Forster, 1929–1960: A Selected Edition*
(University of Missouri Press, 2008), 412.

At last one suggested, "This sounds like a job for Austin Grimes"—a new technician, hungry for any work. Austin arrived to find me all too keen to procrastinate writing my dissertation. Watching him remove the piano's front, I felt like a transgressive voyeur into his craft's mysteries. With the mechanism exposed (behold, a wonder), he showed how some hammers' arms were so warped that they were missing the strings entirely—hence the silent keys.

Then he paused and looked me over before confiding: "I'm going to do something I would never do on a regular piano. But given your budget, this is the way to proceed."

He took out a lighter—a lighter!—and waved its flame up and down one of the arms that he was twisting. After a half minute of this singeing, the arm was aligned again, and the hammer hit the strings properly.

"How on earth did you know how to do that?" I gasped. "Did you go to school to become trained?" No, he hadn't. As someone who had been in school almost my entire life, I was dumbfounded.

"So aren't there piano technician schools?" No; there are.

"So why didn't you go to one?"

Austin related that when he had been a chef, he met graduates of prestigious culinary institutes who were unable to handle the demands of a real kitchen. While they'd been trained in all kinds of formal ways, they just didn't have the nuanced sense of the ever-shifting strains of the line.

When Austin decided to change careers, he created his own apprenticeship, rather than enroll in a program. He didn't want to lack a feel for the craft. So he sought out a master piano technician, someone who was willing to take him on for six months of free labor in exchange for free tutelage. Among the strategies he learned was this method with the lighter: the flame's heat expands the moisture in the wooden arm, so after you had twisted it, warmed it, and cooled it, it became "reset" with a new "memory" of its position.

This is the kind of tacit craft knowledge you wouldn't learn in a book. And even if you did, you might not know the right time to apply it. What Austin did was *rhetorical*, insofar as he was judging the occasion (the crappy piano, our miserly fee), and the audience (a collective household that didn't care enough about piano upkeep), and concluding that this was the proper thing to do at this moment. This timeliness, this imaginative use of tools, this dynamic sense of repair, this desire to do something well—this was his craft.

I'm aware that reviving "craft" as a conceit for education risks appearing precious at a moment when far more daunting challenges press upon our classrooms—from outbursts of terrorizing violence to continued savage inequalities in access to schools. And, as design theorist David Pye rued, craft *is a word to start an argument with*.[2]

Nowadays, "craft" tends to evoke either products targeted for niche markets or projects made by hand at home. The former can be abused for marketing ends by corporations whose methods in no way resemble artisanal practices; the latter conveys a diminutive, often gendered sense of isolated production. The title of a recent satire mocks both senses: *How to Sharpen Pencils: A Practical and Theoretical Treatise on the Artisanal Craft of Pencil Sharpening* (2012).

Yet neither connotation captures the scope of the collective practices that suffused skilled labor in Shakespeare's world, where craft was not merely a mechanical process, but also communal, intellectual, physical, emotional. Craft required discipline, enforced by people as well as by the object itself. Its practitioners habituated themselves into ever-evolving patterns. While playmaking was never formalized as a recognized London guild, key features of the theater aligned with craft's dynamic thinking practices.

"Craft" has often been posed in tension with (purportedly) "higher" intellectual pursuits, whether in ancient Greek philosophy, or in the eighteenth-century emergence of "fine arts" discourse, or in disdain for indigenous cultural practices. George Puttenham's rhetorical handbook sought to help sixteenth-century students navigate the path *from the cart to the school, and from thence to the court*; having at last become a courtier, the student must not risk exposing himself as *a craftsman*, who would then be disregarded *with scorn [and] sent back again to the shop*.[3]

Yet the "skills" versus "theory" binary (a rough translation of Aristotle's *techne* versus *episteme*) is more honored in the breach than in the observance. Because *techne* was rendered in Latin as *ars*, it's often Englished as "art." But "craft" is just as viable a translation, as in Chaucer's *The Parliament of Fowls*, which opens with a version of Hippocrates's aphorism *ars longa, vita brevis*—

The lyf so short, the craft so long to lerne

—as well as in scores of Renaissance technical handbooks titled *The Craft of* _____ .

Doing and thinking *are* reciprocal practices. Plato often resorted to craft metaphors to describe intellectual pursuits (such as statecraft), and Aristotle acknowledged that *techne* could involve theoretical reflection upon its own practices. One of Socrates's interlocutors once scoffed at him, *You simply do not stop speaking about shoemakers, fullers, cooks, and doctors, as if our discussion were about them*.[4] Well, they *were* about them: thinking is as much of a craft as any physical trade.

Historians have recovered ways in which "makers' knowledge" was produced by craftspeople working before the Scientific Revolution, yet whose methods yielded genuine empirical insight. For

---

[3] *The Art of English Poesy: A Critical Edition*, ed. Frank Whigham and Wayne A. Rebhorn (Cornell University Press, 2007), 3.25.378–79.
[4] Callicles to Socrates, *Gorgias* (491).

instance, Adriaen Coenen, an unschooled sixteenth-century Dutch fishmonger, kept a "memory book" for over half a century. His chronicles of marine life and tides have proved invaluable to modern biologists.[5]

My friend John Latimer spent his career documenting seasonal changes to flora and fauna along his rural postal delivery route in northern Minnesota. His notebooks spanning four decades track animal migrations, seasonal flowering, changes in the weather. These phenological notes are now being studied by Harvard scientists for evidence of climate change. And the principal investigator of a multimillion-dollar Oak Ridge National Laboratory project had the good sense to overlook what others might dismiss as John's "lack" of advanced degrees, and hired him on account of his extraordinary depth of domain knowledge—knowledge *in the field*.

In short, *making is thinking*.[6] Or, as the editors of the 1623 Folio praised Shakespeare, *His mind and hand went together*. Don't you want yours to go together, too? This kind of mindful *making* applies to everything from a physical object to a philosophical argument. Craft is both cognitive and embodied, as in George Hale's 1614 sword manual, which praises how *the Feete labour equally with the Hands, the Eye and the Judgement walke together*.[7]

The etymology of "craft" reveals that centuries before it becomes a *trade* or *profession* (defended by associated guilds, companies, and unions), it was first a *strength*, a *power*, a *force*. That is, craft meant a physical transformation of some material, as in the earliest instances of resourceful toolmaking. Soon, this capacity to transform becomes isolated as a *skill* or *art*, a dexterous ingenuity.

---

[5] For reproductions of his beautiful sketches, see *The Whale Book: Whales and Other Marine Animals as Described by Adriaen Coenen in 1585* (Reaktion Books, 2003).

[6] Richard Sennett, *The Craftsman* (Yale University Press, 2008), i.

[7] *The Private Schoole of Defence.*

Only later does "crafty" come to mean full of guile—thereby yoking, as Virginia Woolf pointed out, *two incongruous ideas: making useful objects out of solid matter* and *cajolery, cunning, deceit.*[8] Shakespeare deploys "craft" most often in the sense of being *wily*; the solitary instance of the word "craftsmen" in his works appears in King Richard II's scornful dismissal of Bolingbroke's *Wooing poor craftsmen with the craft of smiles* (1.4.28).

Robert Armin, the actor who played Shakespeare's clowns in the early 1600s, toyed with these overlapping senses in the same repeated word (the technical term for which was *antanaclasis*):

> *Craftsmen*, whose *craft* in cleanly covering
> Is to be *crafty* in your kindest cunning[9]

This *cunning* sense of *craft and crafty rub[bing] shoulders*[10] still hints at the cognitive dimension to *making*. There's an intimate, immersive relationship to *material*, whether physical or conceptual. The material resists, pushes back, in a kind of *dialogue with the materials and means of execution.*[11] Craft practitioner Caroline Broadhead calls making *an exchange with materials—what you give to a material, and what it gives back.*[12]

Think of prehistoric caves, where wall contours inspired painters to incorporate *the humps and bulges of the rock to give their images more life and dimension . . . as if some animals were already in the rock, waiting to be revealed by the artist's charcoal and*

---

[8] "Craftsmanship" (April 20, 1937), in *Thoughts on Peace in an Air Raid* (Penguin, 2009).

[9] *Quips upon questions, or, A clownes conceite on occasion offered bewraying a morrallised metamorphoses of changes vpon interrogatories* (1600). In one of the earliest books that could now be considered an English dictionary, Thomas Elyot defined "Techna" as *a craft, also a wyle, or subtyl meane* (1538).

[10] Margaret Atwood reviewing Lewis Hyde's *Trickster Makes This World, Los Angeles Times*, January 25, 1998, 4.

[11] Claude Lévi-Strauss, *The Savage Mind* (University of Chicago Press, 1966), 29.

[12] Answering the question *What is Craft?*: http://r-kelly1316-dc.blogspot.com/2015/11/what-is-craft.html.

paint.[13] Artists describe the process of creation in similar terms: as if the material had an innate form that they *released*. As the eighteenth-century essayist Joseph Addison (alluding to Aristotle) phrased it,

> a Statue lies hid in a Block of Marble; and . . . the Art of the Statuary only clears away the superfluous Matter, and removes the Rubbish. The Figure is in the Stone, the Sculptor only finds it.[14]

Richard Sennett speculates that the experience of an object's material resistance serves as practice for working with resistance in the social realm, where you must determine where your influence lies (where you can push, where you must give in). C. Wright Mills went even further, suggesting that a craftsperson *forms his own self as he works toward the perfection of his craft*.[15]

Again, Addison: *What sculpture is to a block of marble, education is to a human soul.*

The crafter transforms a common object into her own artifact. She has made something that *was* public into something private, her own—the way a block of stone ceases to belong to nature and becomes the sculptor's as she works on it.[16] In the process, a recurrent set of physical habits evolves, and, with them, habits of mind, to which the crafter can return.

In this sense, craft becomes both empirical and cumulative. Such habits, in turn, can be shared with others, tried and evaluated by them, in a public component: a recursive sense of *proving* the

[13] Chip Walter, "First Artists," *National Geographic*, January 2015, 57.

[14] *Spectator*, no. 215 (November 6, 1711). This passage, along with thousands of others, can be found on Brad Pasanek's "helter-skelter anthology," *The Mind Is a Metaphor*: http:// metaphors.iath.virginia.edu/metaphors/10705.

[15] "On Intellectual Craftsmanship," in *The Sociological Imagination* (Oxford, 1959), 196.

[16] David Lowenthal, *The Past Is a Foreign Country—Revisited* (Cambridge, 2015), 85; citing the sixteenth-century educator Johannes Sturm, *De imitatione*, who in turn was citing Horace: *publica materies privati iuris erit. Ars poetica* (131).

craft, and thereby *im-proving* it. This is "quality control" from within, by peers who understand the domain.

Over time, these skills become consolidated as a kind of "grammar" of strategies, shared within a community, communicated across generations. When someone is undertaking meaningful work, *the thoughts of the men of past ages guide [their] hands.*[17] Experienced members initiate novices. While its tacit patterns can be made into formulas, "craft" resists verbal description.

Even when its "secrets" are published, the practice itself requires—well, *practice*. Its difficult-to-codify habits are best transmitted in person, through modeling, observation, imitation, correction, adjustment. Incorporating this body of knowledge, learning how to improvise within constraints, appreciating how limited resources shape solutions to problems—this is apprenticeship.

Apprenticeship gets a bad rap these days. For one thing, we hold out no certain prospect of employment at the end of training, as the early modern system of labor did. (Though already by 1621 Robert Burton was griping that while *Most other trades and professions after some seaven yeares prentiship, are enabled by their craft to live of themselves. . . . Only Schollers, me thinks are most uncertaine, unrespected, subject to all casualties, and hazards.*)[18]

Real apprenticeship takes time. It demands pauses, and repeated exercises to judge progress, propose next steps. While craft must be future oriented (in terms of perfecting its object), and draw upon past experience, it unfolds in the present, *a conversation flowing through time*, in woodworker Peter Korn's resonant phrase.[19] You learn *why* your models make certain kinds of moves, so that you can emulate them, and eventually surpass them.

Apprenticeship also requires a space in which it can unfold: the

[17] William Morris, *Useful Work versus Useless Toil* (Socialist League Office, 1886), 21.
[18] *The Anatomy of Melancholy*, 130–31.
[19] *Why We Make Things and Why It Matters* (David Godine, 2013), 31.

schoolroom, the workshop, the studio, the theater. As Christopher Alexander writes, *Treat each small work group, in every kind of industry and office, as a place of learning—master and apprentices.*[20] Places provide a focal point for practiced attention.

Finally, apprenticeship entails judgment, discrimination, and evaluation—and produces "the joys of craft":

> In craftsmanship there is a continuous movement back and forth between usefulness and beauty; this back-and-forth motion has a name: pleasure. Things are pleasing because they are useful and beautiful.[21]

Craft takes place in a collaborative environment where skill is honed, in conjunction with others. This space is distinguished by gradations of expertise, as *knowledge is continually being refined, enriched, or completely revised by experience.*[22] Total expertise is always deferred; *We are all apprentices in a craft where no one ever becomes a master.*[23]

Yet there *are* degrees of earned authority, much as some now resent this fact. (My retired colleague Jenny Brady once received this indignant student evaluation: *She thinks she knows more than we do!*)

The practice—the tradition—is handed over, as an inheritance that must be earned. And while we speak today about a "masterpiece" as the ultimate product of your career, in the apprentice system a "masterpiece" instead was the somewhat bizarre-looking object proving that you could do every task demanded by the craft. Only then were you ready to go on, ready to become an autono-

[20] *A Pattern Language* (Oxford University Press, 1977), 83.
[21] Octavio Paz, "Seeing and Using: Art and Craftsmanship," in *Convergences: Essays on Art and Literature* (Harcourt Brace Jovanovich, 1987), 58. See the chapter "The Joys of Craft" by computer programmer Fred Brooks in *The Mythical Man Month: Essays on Software Engineering* (Addison-Wesley, 1975), 23–24.
[22] Charles and Janet Dixon Keller, "Thinking and Acting with Iron," in *Understanding Practice*, ed. Jean Lave and Seth Chaiklin (Cambridge University Press, 1993), 127.
[23] Ernest Hemingway, *New York Journal-American*, July 11, 1961.

mous (a self-directed) practitioner. The "masterpiece" is akin to a school's "commencement"—the beginning, not the end.

Shakespeare's play*making* extended the dramaturgical experiments of earlier craft guilds:

> The craftsman's 'form' is learnt in the process of making, by innumerable examples, not by recipe and precept. He works like a good cook. 'Take of fennel and cast in enough' say those maddening cookery books of Shakespeare's time. Familiarity and habituation; the long maturing of a seven years' apprenticeship made a craftsman.
>
> The craft of making poetry and of making plays had long been familiar to Englishmen. It was a 'gentle' craft—like woodcraft or working fine metals.[24]

This conceit was prevalent during his lifetime. Even Ben Jonson, who took pains to compliment Shakespeare backhandedly as a "natural" poet, depicts his predecessor hammering out his words like Hephaestus, the ur-craftsperson, "famous for his skill":

> Who casts to write a living line must sweat,
> . . . and strike the second heat
> Upon the Muses' anvil.[25]

Elsewhere, Jonson provides a definition of "poesy" that harkens back to its Greek roots in the word for "maker":

> A poem, as I have told you, is the work of the poet; the end and fruit of his labour and study. Poesy is his skill or craft of making; the very fiction itself, the reason or form of the work.[26]

---

[24] Muriel Clara Bradbrook, *Shakespeare, the Craftsman* (Cambridge University Press, 1969), 75.

[25] "To the Memory of My Beloved Master William Shakespeare, and What He Hath Left Us," from the prefatory materials to the 1623 Folio, lines 59–61.

[26] *Timber, or Discoveries*, in *Ben Jonson*, vol. 8, *The Poems; The Prose Works*, ed. C. H. Herford, P. Simpson, and E. Simpson (Oxford University Press, 1947), 636.

Craft of making—that's how to think like Shakespeare and his *fine filed phrase.*[27]

Or, even better: *craft of will,*[28] a finely filed phrase that distills the maker's mark with both aim and name.

---

[27] Frances Meres, *Palladis Tamia, Wits Treasury* (1598). Contrast Shakespeare's modestly apologizing for his "unpolished lines" in his dedication to *Venus and Adonis.*

[28] *A Lover's Complaint*, line 126.

MAD FASHIONs,

OD FASHIONS,

All out of Fashions,

OR,

The Emblems of these Distracted times.

By *Iohn Taylor.*

LONDON,

Printed by *Iohn Hammond,* for *Thomas Banks,* 1642.

John Taylor, MAD FASHIONS, OD FASHIONS, *All out of Fashions, OR, The Emblems of these Distracted Times* (London: John Hammond, 1642).

4

OF FIT

A word fitly spoken is like apples of
gold in pictures of silver.
—Proverbs 25:11, 1611 translation

Cicero nailed it: nothing is more difficult than to see what is fit, in both life and words.[1] Educators have always fretted over what is "fit," and struggled with how to articulate (not to mention transmit) it. "Fitness," or congruence between behavior and expectations, demands a deft awareness of ever-evolving circumstances: audience, place, resources, occasion (what the Greeks termed *kairos*—which also could mean mark, or target). As John Bury, the Tudor translator of Isocrates's *Orations*, exhorted: we must *learn how to behave ourselves to all degrees, and how in all times and tempests also to dispose us.*[2]

I'd rather not recount the times I've been told I didn't "fit" a particular opportunity, whether personal or professional. It feels alienating, and downright unfair, because it seems as though there are no clear-cut criteria for what counts as "fit."

Yet as readers, we have all experienced an exhilaration when encountering something so well phrased that it strikes us as convincing: it is *altogether fitting and proper.*[3] As Alexander Pope

---

[1] *De oratore* (69–70): *Ut enim in vita sic in oratione nihil est difficilius quam quid deceat videre.*

[2] Cited in Lacey Baldwin Smith, *Treason in Tudor England: Politics and Paranoia* (Princeton University Press, 1966), 87.

[3] Abraham Lincoln, Gettysburg Address; he returns to that phrase "fitting and proper" in the Second Inaugural as well.

wrote in his *Essay on Criticism* (1711), *True wit is nature to advantage dressed, / What oft was thought, but ne'er so well expressed* (97–98).

Such phrasings are often more than apt. They enhance our understanding, taking us beyond *what oft was thought* through sheer clarity. We have the impression of grasping a truth that had eluded us. Something about the wording carries us with it, enables us to transcend.

Pope separates thought and expression (a binary enacted in the balanced structure of his couplet). Yet wording isn't solely a dress of thought. Pope's ideal is a work where all is *just or fit* (294): *just*, as in *just so*, exact . . . right in every way, *woven so fit*.[4]

But what does he mean by *fit*? Pope's reference to "dress" may help. Shakespeare and his contemporaries emerged from the culture of the handicraft trades, often concerned with fashion and clothing. Here, "fit" could mean the palpable difference between penury and profit.

Shakespeare would first have been exposed to a handicraft environment in his own home, in a glover's workshop. He grew up in an artisanal household, from English society's middle ranks. So did most of his fellow writers: George Peele's father was a salter; Anthony Munday's, a draper; Henry Chettle's, a dyer; Robert Greene's, a saddler. Thomas Lodge's father was a grocer; Ben Jonson's stepfather, a bricklayer; Thomas Middleton was exposed to both of these trades, with his stepfather a grocer, and his father a bricklayer. Edmund Spenser's father was likely a journeyman clothmaker, and Gabriel Harvey was the son of a ropemaker—much to the merriment of his scathing adversary Thomas Nashe:

[4] Those are Ben Jonson's lines, in praise of Shakespeare:
  Nature herself was proud of his designs,
    And joyed to wear the dressing of his lines,
  Which were so richly spun, and woven so fit,
    As, since, she will vouchsafe no other wit.
"To the Memory of My Beloved Master William Shakespeare, and What He Hath Left Us," from the prefatory materials to the 1623 Folio, lines 47–50.

Had I a Ropemaker to my father, & somebody had cast it in my teeth, I would forthwith have writ in praise of Ropemakers, & proved it by solid syllogistry to be one of the 7. liberal sciences.[5]

Christopher Marlowe's father rose to become treasurer of the Shoemaker's Company. Making shoes was the artisanal practice that most resembled making gloves. (In German, the word for "glove" is *Handschuh*—"hand-shoe.") Both trades worked with leather, requiring similar labor-intensive techniques: stretching, drying, tanning, dying, cutting, stitching, embellishing. And they would have reeked—both urine and excrement were used in the curing process (as my kids found out when their noses were assaulted by the pungent SMELL THIS! boxes at Stratford-upon-Avon).

In the first stage of this process, a large round knife would scrape the leather—a tool recalled by Shakespeare: *Does he not wear a great round beard like a glover's paring-knife?*[6] Raw materials needed to be treated in careful stages before their ultimate transformation into consumer products. To reduce wastage, they had to be careful in their cut.

Many virtues could have been habituated in the workshop: efficiency; foresight; coordination of multiple steps in an evolving process; a kind of "feel" for the product. Such a household would have introduced a child to an entire vocabulary and community, later recalled with evident pride:

FIRST REBEL. Oh miserable age! Virtue is not regarded in handicraftsmen.

SECOND REBEL. The nobility think scorn to go in leather aprons.[7]

I suspect Shakespeare also learned the old real estate saw about *location, location, location*[8]: the powerful glovers boasted some of the key stalls in Stratford's market.

[5] *The Works of Thomas Nashe*, vol. 1, ed. Ronald B. McKerrow (A. H. Bullen, 1903), 270.
[6] *The Merry Wives of Windsor* (1.4.17–18).
[7] *2 Henry VI* (4.2.10–12).
[8] Demosthenes is said to have insisted that the three most important things in oratory

The market for fashion requires a feel for timing—for when something is out of fashion, it might be *richly suited but unsuitable*.[9] Knowledge matters—not only of the market, but of the customers' bodies, down to their fingers, toes, even their personalities. As Bernard Shaw's Tanner complains about people not recognizing his changed life:

> The only man who behaved sensibly was my tailor; he took my measurements anew every time he saw me, while all the rest went on with their old measurements and expected them to fit me.[10]

This is "fitting" to figures, like the bespoke roles Shakespeare would later develop for specific members of his company, *fitted to the person*.[11] The trickster Autolycus knows so well how to size up his songs to his duped marks that he can sell them better than any milliner *can so fit his customers with gloves*.[12] Elsewhere, in sonnet 111, there's the sense that the craft itself shapes the creator: *my nature is subdued / To what it works in, like the dyer's hand*.

Against the conventional fantasy that creativity explodes out of emotion or passion, David Byrne confirms that we *make work to fit preexisting formats*:

> the tailoring process—form being tailored to fit a given context—is largely unconscious, instinctive. . . . Genius—the emergence of a truly remarkable and memorable work—seems to appear when a thing is perfectly suited to its context. . . . When the right thing is in the right place, we are moved. . . . [Art is putting things] into prescribed forms or squeezing them into new forms that perfectly fit some emerging context.[13]

---

were "delivery," "delivery," and "delivery." Plutarch, *The Lives of the Ten Orators*, ed. Harold North Fowler (Harvard University Press, 1960), 419.

[9] *All's Well That Ends Well* (1.1.146).

[10] *Man and Superman: A Comedy and a Philosophy* (Brentano's, 1922), 37.

[11] *fitted to the person*, Sir Richard Baker, *Theatrum Redivivum* (1662), cited by Tiffany Stern, "Production Processes," in *The Cambridge Guide to the Worlds of Shakespeare*, ed. Bruce R. Smith (Cambridge University Press, 2016), 123.

[12] *The Winter's Tale* (4.4.190–91).

[13] *How Music Works* (McSweeney's, 2012), 29.

What is good fit? *Bad* fit is easy to recognize, whether someone's *not fit* for a task or out of shape (or both). In *Cymbeline*, the cloddish Cloten presumes that because the garments of another character "fit" him, *Why should his mistress, who was made by him that made the tailor, not be fit too?*[14] The illustration to this chapter depicts a mis-fit man, his boots on his hands and his gloves on his feet. The world is turned upside down, with the cart before the horse, and *the cat had the dire disaster / To be worried by the mouse.*[15] In contrast, cataloging all of the traits that constitute *good* fit is impossible. Yet we still experience the sensation of good fit, the intangible but real *ensemble* between form and context—that *right*ness that Byrne describes, or the *fit audience* Milton sought for his writing, like a hand in a glove.[16]

Gloves throughout Shakespeare's plays can be tokens of love, status, vows, and conflict. Their prosthetic intimacy conveys an intimate fusion between subject and object, as when Romeo yearns to be *a glove upon that hand, / That I might touch that cheek!*[17]

Addressing her sleeve as a love token, Cressida envisions Troilus

> thinking in his bed
> Of thee and me, and sighs, and takes my glove,
> And gives memorial dainty kisses to it,
> As I kiss thee.[18]

Richard Barnfield's charming sonnet tells a "sweet boy" to

> place this glove near thy heart,
> Wear it, and lodge it still within thy breast,

---

[14] *Julius Caesar* (2.1.153); *Cymbeline* (4.1.3–4).

[15] That's from Victorian poet William Brighty Rands's "Topsyturvey-World," set to music by Natalie Merchant on *Leave Your Sleep* (2010).

[16] Christopher Alexander, *Notes on the Synthesis of Form* (Harvard University Press, 1964), 16–18; *Paradise Lost* (7.31), in *The Complete Poetry and Essential Prose of John Milton*, ed. William Kerrigan, John Rumrich, and Stephen M. Fallon (Modern Library, 2007).

[17] *Romeo and Juliet* (2.1.66–67).

[18] *Troilus and Cressida* (5.2.77–80).

When the boy replies *How can that be? . . . A glove is for the hand not for the heart*, Barnfield unstitches his puzzle:

> 'If thou from glove dost take away the g,
> Then glove is love: and so I send it thee.'[19]

The rhetorical analogue to this fitness between subject and object was *decorum*: determining the level of style *apt and agreeable* to the person, place, and moment.[20] Aristotle called this *correspondence to subject*; Milton thought decorum was *the grand masterpiece to observe*. Leon Battista Alberti applied the notion to architecture: *To every Member [of a building] therefore ought to be allotted its fit place and proper situation*.[21]

William Hogarth held "fitness" in such high esteem that he devoted the first chapter of his treatise on beauty to it: *Fitness of the parts to the design . . . is of the greatest consequence to the beauty of the whole*.[22] I've found that *part-to-whole* notion one of the most evasive, yet most essential aspects of teaching reading. Again, there's no rule for identifying it, but you can feel it. Learning to think means picking up that "feel," akin to a baker's awareness of the consistency of dough, a doctor's gentle pressure on the patient's body, a sailor's hand on the tiller. All of these touches are developed through emulation for "fit."

The Elizabethan George Puttenham suggested two English synonyms for *decorum*:

---

[19] Sonnet 14 from *Cynthia* (1595).

[20] Thomas Wilson, *The Arte of Rhetorique* (1560), ed. George Herbert Mair (Clarendon Press, 1909), 170.

[21] Aristotle, *Rhetoric* (3.7), ed. Frederick Solmsen (Modern Library, 1954), 178; *Milton's Tractate on Education* (1673), ed. Oscar Browning (Cambridge University Press, 1883), 16; Leon Battista Alberti, *On Building* (1485), in *The Emergence of Modern Architecture: A Documentary History from 1000 to 1810*, ed. Liane Lefaivre and Alexander Tzonis (Routledge, 2004), 57.

[22] *Analysis of Beauty* (1753), in Lefaivre and Tzonis, *Emergence of Modern Architecture*, 330. Hogarth echoes Andrea Palladio, who similarly underlines how beauty
> will derive from . . . the relationship of the whole to the parts, and of the parts among themselves and to the whole.
The Four Books on Architecture (1570), trans. Robert Tavernor and Richard Schofield (MIT Press, 2002), 7.

seemliness, that is to say, for his good shape and utter [outward] appearance well pleasing the eye. We call it also *comeliness* for the delight it bringeth coming towards us.[23]

Others termed this *decency, meetness, grace, propriety*. No matter what we call it, "fit" is as necessary to tailor a word as it is to tailor a fabric. As Philip Sidney says in his first sonnet to *Astrophil and Stella* (1591): *I sought fit words*.

There's no such thing as "one size fits all" in the craft of thinking. In *All's Well That Ends Well,* the Countess scoffs that the Clown couldn't have an *answer that fits all questions . . . like a barber's chair that fits all buttocks*. She skeptically concludes: *It must be an answer of most monstrous size that must fit all demands*. Even acting should be *aptly fitted*: *suit the action to the word, the word to the action.*[24]

While "personalized learning" is the latest ed-tech buzz, in practice it means de*person*alized learning, via algorithmic surveillance at remote screens.[25] True tailoring comes from teachers who know the needs and potential and aspirations of their students—and who have the time to adjust, to fit the task to the student, the student to the task.

The language-fits-like-leather conceit is made explicit by Feste: *A sentence is but a chev'rel glove to a good wit. How quickly the wrong side may be turned outward.* Elsewhere in Shakespeare, the malleability of material is spoken of as *cheverel conscience . . . you might please to stretch it*, or as *a wit of cheverel, that stretches from an inch*

[23] *The Art of English Poesie* (1589), ed. Frank Whigham and Wayne A. Rebhorn (Cornell University Press, 2007), 348.

[24] *All's Well That Ends Well* (2.2.14–32); *The Taming of the Shrew* (Induction.83); *Hamlet* (3.2.16–17).

[25] Here are just four articles that make visceral the impoverished vision of the ed-tech industry: Michael Godsey, "The Deconstruction of the K-12 Teacher: When Kids Can Get Their Lessons from the Internet, What's Left for Classroom Instructors to Do?" *Atlantic*, March 25, 2015; Kristina Rizganov, "Inside Silicon Valley's Big-Money Push to Remake American Education," *Mother Jones*, November 3, 2017; Nellie Bowles, "Silicon Valley Came to Kansas Schools. That Started a Rebellion," *New York Times*, April 21, 2019; Jared Woodard, "Rotten STEM: How Technology Corrupts Education," *American Affairs Journal*, August 2019.

narrow to an ell broad!—what we might now call the elastic, plastic nature of cognition.[26] The notion itself was proverbial—*he hath a conscience like a cheveril's skin*[27]—and Shakespeare stretched it to suit his own purposes. A practiced craftsperson finds ways to turn something into a kind of second skin, exhibiting *the contours of the handiness it conceals.*[28]

When Renaissance courtiers sought to act with grace, they tried to act as if they weren't *trying* to act: *Not to exhibit craft, but rather to submerge it.*[29] A fancy term for this is *sprezzatura*, or a kind of artful artlessness, following the precept of Michelangelo: *Take infinite pains to make something that looks effortless.*[30] As W. B. Yeats knew:

> A line will take us hours maybe;
> Yet if it does not seem a moment's thought,
> Our stitching and unstitching has been naught.[31]

Examine any draft manuscript, and you see what Yeats means. The final product may appear seamless, but untold hours have been devoted to making the stitching invisible.

I love those subtle moments when Shakespearean characters seem to be tinkering with their own thoughts, to make them better fit the moment. Think of when Richard II imagines for himself *a little grave*, which he revises into *A little, little grave*—what a delicate diminution. Or when Prospero proclaims that the grandiose wedding pageant he has just blown the special effects budget on is *melted into air*—and then, as if to capture the reverie at the insubstantiality of it floating away, restitches this as *into thin air.*[32] I'm reminded of Francis Quarles's 1643 emblem:

---

[26] *Twelfth Night* (3.1.10–11); *Henry VIII* (2.3.32–33); *Romeo and Juliet* (2.3.76–77).

[27] See John Ray, *A compleat collection of English proverbs* (1670).

[28] Harry Berger, Jr., *The Absence of Grace* (Stanford University Press, 2000), 11.

[29] Andrew Wyeth (1943), in Eric Protter, *Painters on Painting* (Grosset & Dunlap, 1971), 257.

[30] Cited in F. L. Lucas, *Style: The Art of Writing Well* (1956; Harriman House Limited, 2012), 43.

[31] "Adam's Curse" (1904), lines 4–6.

[32] *Richard II* (3.3.153–54); *The Tempest* (4.1.150). We call this *diacope*—a form of repeti-

> My soul, what's lighter than a feather? Wind.
> Than wind? The fire. And what, than fire? The mind.
> What's lighter than the mind? A thought. Than thought?
> This bubble world. What than this bubble? Nought.[33]

Thinking transpires in front of you, as the thought floats away, into air—into thin air.

Or we might otherwise consider "fitting," in the context of writing, the practice of bringing things together. The word "apt" (another early modern synonym for "fit") derives from the root *apere*, a verb meaning to fit things together, in the manner of a carpenter, joiner, weaver, bellows mender, tinker, tailor (all trades in *Midsummer Night's Dream*). Like teaching, like writing, like thinking, these crafts all require pliability, threading things in the right place, at the right time, and thereby strengthening them.

Already during Shakespeare's lifetime, verses were attributed to him that we know weren't written by him. (By the eighteenth century, *relics* began to be attributed to him too—even Shakespeare's purported gloves!)[34] One such ditty was found in the miscellany by Sir Francis Fane:

> The gift is small,
> The will is all,
> Alexander Aspinall.[35]

The apocryphal story goes that Aspinall, the Stratford schoolmaster, bought gloves from the Shakespeare workshop in 1594, and that Shakespeare composed these verses for Aspinall's bride. *The only gift is a portion of thyself*, proclaimed Emerson; *Hence the fitness of beautiful, not useful things for gifts.*[36]

---

tion with an intervening word. See Sister Miriam Joseph, *Shakespeare's Use of the Arts of Language* (1947; Paul Dry Books, 2008), 86–88.

[33] *Emblemes* (1643), 19.

[34] Johanne M. Stochholm, *Garrick's Folly* (Routledge, 2015), 24.

[35] *The Oxford Companion to Shakespeare*, ed. Michael Dobson, Stanley Wells, Will Sharpe, and Erin Sullivan (Oxford University Press, 2015), 17.

[36] "Gifts" (1844).

À l'École (At the School), 1910. Villemard, Chromolithographie, Paris, Bibliothèque nationale de France.

5

OF PLACE

[Place] is the first of all things.
—Archytas of Tarentum (c. 375 BCE)

Shakespeare's school was a place. It was a place where he studied with other people, of different ages. These people studied in the same place, at the same time.

It's hard to imagine a more banal statement! Yet this "old-fashioned" scenario runs counter to breathless demands to demolish "conventional" classrooms, disaggregate the "components" of education, and "free" ourselves into remote, asynchronous fora. It's as if we were driven by Descartes's fantasy that a person could become *a substance whose whole essence or nature is only that of thinking, and which, in order to exist, has no need of any place.*[1]

Less than a decade ago, heady ed-tech reformers like Sebastian Thrun were asserting that *there will be only 10 institutions in the world delivering higher education* by the mid-twenty-first century.[2] But hardly a year later, Thrun had to concede that massive open online courses were a *lousy product: We're not doing anything as rich and powerful as what a traditional liberal-arts education would offer you.* In response to his company's chronic failure to provide free remedial education, it pivoted to paid corporate train-

---

[1] *Discourse on Method* (1637), cited in Bernard Williams, *Descartes* (Penguin, 1978), 109.

[2] Steven Leckart, "The Stanford Education Experiment That Could Change Higher Learning Forever," *Wired*, March 20, 2012.

ing—the opposite of what Udacity had set out to do.[3] Now *that's* audacity.

Advocates of distance have always pined for a day when mediated systems could escape the tired confines of face-to-face instruction. In their ideal world, bold technologies will make it possible for dispersed pupils to enroll, with administrators (or, better yet, algorithms) assessing them from afar. New pedagogical tools are claimed to be not only more affordable than traditional classes, but also more effective.

According to one prominent expert, the average distance learner *knows more of the subject, and knows it better, than the student who has covered the same ground in the classroom. . . . the day is coming when the work done [via distance learning] will be greater in amount than that done in the class-rooms of our colleges.* The future of education will be here at last!

These quotations come from 1885, from Yale classicist (and future University of Chicago president) William Rainey Harper, praising *correspondence courses.*[4] That's right: you've got (snail) mail. Journalist Nicholas Carr has chronicled the indefatigable boosterism about mass-mediated education: the phonograph, instructional radio, televised lectures, the fill-in-the-blank worksheet.[5] All were heralded as transformative media in their day. This should give us pause whenever the latest iteration of distance learning recurs. Are taped talks and online chat rooms the sum of an education?

I concede that watching a recording of an enthralling lecturer could surpass a mediocre speaker in a large hall where many are dozing; "distance learning" begins in the second row. Yet I persist in doubting that students *watch* an online lecture with the attention it demands. They're just not in the same *place* with the

[3] Mark Chafkin, "Udacity's Sebastian Thrun, Godfather of Free Online Education, Changes Course," *Fast Company*, November 14, 2013.

[4] Cited with approbation by Michael Simonson and Deborah J. Seepersaud in *Distance Education: Definition and Glossary of Terms* (Information Age Publishing, 2018), 8.

[5] "The Prehistory of the MOOC": http://www.roughtype.com/?p=1892.

teacher—physically, temporally, cognitively. Their attention is not held. And, as studies have alarmingly confirmed, distance learning is least helpful for those already disadvantaged: first-generation students; language learners; those from families without access to technology.[6]

At its best, education is a dynamic and interactive conversation between a student motivated to think harder and a demanding teacher—they fit together, in that same place. That's been the formula for three thousand years, and it's unlikely to change anytime soon. It may be that you don't need this kind of education for *training*. But how keen are you to cross a bridge designed by someone who has only earned online badges, or have your appendix removed by a surgeon who hasn't had to defend her practice in person to the chief of her department?

A Columbia University neuroscientist, Stuart Firestein, became discouraged by students regurgitating his lectures without internalizing the complexity of scientific inquiry. To combat this trend, Firestein invited his colleagues to visit his seminar to discuss what they *don't* know. As Firestein concluded, it is informed ignorance, not information, that generates real knowledge.[7] Mere data transmission doesn't induce deep learning. It's the ability to interact, to think hard thoughts *in the presence* of other people.

Even Coursera cofounder Andrew Ng had to admit that the real value of an education *isn't just the content. . . . The real value is the interactions with professors and other, equally bright students.*[8] Jacques Barzun was even more blunt: *There is unfortunately no method or gimmick that will replace teaching. We have seen the failure of one method after another . . . Teaching will not change; it is a hand-to-hand, face-to-face encounter.*[9]

[6] Spiros Protopsaltis and Sandy Baum ask, "Does Online Education Live Up to Its Promise?" (2019): https://mason.gmu.edu/~sprotops/OnlineEd.pdf.

The answer? No.

[7] *Ignorance: How It Drives Science* (Oxford University Press, 2012).

[8] Will Oremus, "The New Public Ivies," *Slate*, July 18, 2012.

[9] Preface to the 1983 edition of *Teacher in America* (1945): http://www.the-rathouse.com/JacquesBarzunPreface.html.

To state the obvious: there's a human aspect to education, what John Henry Newman once called *the living voice, the breathing form, the expressive countenance.*[10] This isn't distance learning; it's *close learning*: the laborious, time-consuming, and irreplaceable proximity between teacher and student.

(I just googled "proximity learning" and was dismayed to find it's the Orwellian name of a corporation that serves as a *temp agency for hiring online teachers.* You can't make this stuff up.)

Our word "school" derives from the Greek *skhole*—"leisure." *Skhole*, in turn, goes back to the Indo-European root **segh*: seize, hold, pause. Both "pause" and "leisure" sound a bit odd to us; we tend to associate school with *work*. But "school" was a particular kind of *activity*, one that demanded a respite from physical necessity, in order to pursue thoughts in common—a freedom to think and interact alongside other human beings. Political philosopher Michael Oakeshott says we miss something fundamental if we don't *think of [school] as a place . . . a home of learning.*[11]

Now, Shakespeare liked to jest about how reluctantly children go to school, and how eagerly they hasten away, as Romeo laments:

Love goes toward love as schoolboys from their books,
But love from love toward school with heavy looks.[12]

While Shakespeare caricatures schoolmasters, the mockery seems appreciative to me—the sign of *a playwright and an audience who felt assured enough of the value of learning to be amused at the foibles and excesses of its less balanced admirers.*[13] There's even a seventeenth-century anecdote that Shakespeare *had been in his younger yeares a Schoolmaster in the Countrey,*[14] perhaps with as few as a dozen

---

[10] "What Is a University?" in *Rise and Progress of Universities and Benedictine Essays* (Basil Montague Pickering, 1873), 14.

[11] *The Voice of Liberal Learning* (Yale, 1989), 97.

[12] *Romeo and Juliet* (2.2.198–99).

[13] M. H. Curtis, "Education and Apprenticeship," *Shakespeare Survey* 17 (1964): 57.

[14] John Aubrey (*Brief Lives*, 1681), citing William Beeston, the son of theatrical man Christopher Beeston, who acted with Shakespeare in *Every Man in His Humour* (1598).

students. Before the advent of professional drama in London, many plays were composed by schoolmasters.

His Stratford school wasn't much larger, with perhaps forty boys enrolled. An illustration from a 1573 catechism depicts a conventional arrangement, with rows of facing benches. It's easy to disdain such formality, from the teacher's throne-like chair (the oft-scorned "sage on the stage") to the menacing birch rods at his feet. Yet are today's glossy images of students bathed in the isolated glow of their separate screens any better? Those students might be in the same room together, but are they in the same *place*?

They are living out the horrifying vision of futuristic techno-pedagogy satirized in the 1910 French postcard at the head of this chapter. As the instructor dumps books into the hopper, an assistant grinds them up to deposit their wisdom into the pupils' passive ears: *content delivery!* When I look at that postcard, Gertrude Stein's quip about Oakland comes to mind: *there's no there*.[15] The people are not present to one another, in that mutual space. They are absented. They might as well be anywhere.

We all know that teachers are best able to devote intensive attention to students when classes are humanely scaled, and where proximity generates trust.[16] But the clearest confirmation is that wealthy educational reformers have always sent their *own* children to schools with small classes, so that they might experience the free play of mind denied to others.

Small physical classrooms emerge from a long heritage of "thinking spaces" that provide an anchor in space and time. The Athenian Peripatos; medieval guildhalls; the early modern academy; the Enlightenment salon and coffee shop; the German research seminar; the American Lyceum; the "Flying University"

---

[15] *Everybody's Autobiography* (Knopf, 1937), 298.

[16] My college roommate Garrett Delavan has written an essay titled "Why Our Kids Must and Can Get Smaller Schools and Classes," in *The Teacher's Attention* (Temple University Press, 2009). Diane Whitmore Schanzenbach concludes that yes, no matter what technocrats try to tell you, class size *does* matter: http://nepc.colorado.edu/files/pb _-_class_size.pdf.

movement that educated the likes of Marie Curie—all were dynamic gatherings that benefited from an intimate scale.

"College" itself derived from *collegium*, the Roman legal category for a partnership united in common purpose. Cultural institutions—schools, libraries, museums, archives—are all hubs where the roots of the past are not only stored, but made available for new interpretations and rearrangements: brain, body, and environment working in concert to develop our minds.

Today's cognitive science validates what memory practitioners already knew in Shakespeare's era: physical configurations reinforce recollection, whether on the page of a book or on the stage of a theater. A grisly anecdote relates the origins of mnemonic practices: The Greek poet Simonides had just stepped outside a banqueting hall when the roof collapsed. Mutilated corpses could be identified only by Simonides's recollection of their places around the table—an insight that generated an entire art of memory through spatial association.

They even called this the method of *loci*, or "places." In our haste to adopt dis-embodied, placeless education, we obliterate this insight. Asynchronous classes further obliterate the power of carving out a communal place in *time*. The endless immediacy of digital fora precludes *the gift of the interval*:[17] the space to think.

The college where I teach relocated to its urban Memphis campus in 1925. At that time, nearly the entire student body could fit inside the auditorium. My neighbor John Curry attended school here in the 1940s. Whenever he returns to that same auditorium for an event, memories well up within him from the last seven decades. As if he were walking into Simonides's classical memory palace, this place is superimposed with layer upon layer of past communities, a *chronological connectivity* in living continuity with the present.[18] As Petrarch wrote to a

[17] Oakeshott, *Voice of Liberal Learning*, 127.
[18] James Howard Kunstler, *Home from Nowhere* (Touchstone Press, 1998), 89.

friend, *There was present in every step something that inspired both our voices and our minds.*[19]

Will online badge earners say the same thing seventy years from now?

Hannah Arendt made the centrality of *place* for society vivid by likening it to sitting around a table:

> To live together in the world means essentially that a world of things is between those who have it in common, as the table is located between those who sit around it, the world like every in-between relates and separates men at the same time. What makes mass society so difficult to bear is . . . the fact that the world between them has lost its power to gather them together, to relate and to separate them. The weirdness of this situation resembles a spiritual séance where a number of people gathered around a table might suddenly, through some magic trick, see the table vanish from their midst, so that two persons sitting opposite each other were no longer separated but also would be entirely unrelated to each other by anything tangible.[20]

Think of the scene in *The Tempest* where Ariel deceives the ship-wrecked crew with a mirage-like banquet on a table—before making the banquet vanish. It's *a quaint device*, as the Folio's stage directions term it: a trick (3.3.53). But the trick exposes how vulnerable we feel without something in common between us: a book, a sanctuary, a stage, a table are all tools for conviviality.[21] They provide a focal point for practiced attention, where making of the highest human kind can take place.

Except now it's not just the table—the notion of place itself is being pulled out from under us. *This is no place* (*As You Like It* 2.3.27).

---

[19] *Familiares* (6.2.5), trans. Timothy Kircher, in *The Poet's Wisdom* (Brill, 2005), 38–39.

[20] *The Human Condition* (1958; University of Chicago Press, 1998), 53.

[21] See Ivan Illich, *Tools for Conviviality* (Harper & Row, 1973).

Angie and Me, © Eric Pickersgill, 2015, from the series *Removed*.

6
OF ATTENTION

distraction is the enemy of all education
—Immanuel Kant, *On Education* (1803)

On the ground floor of my office building, I'm pointing out the details of a wall map to my children. The bell rings, classes let out. I mutter an easy prediction: *Watch this: everyone will stare at their phones.* Students amble into the hallway. One meanders toward us, bumps into me, recalibrates her trajectory without looking up, and continues her Roomba-like textwalking. My kids giggle.

I'm no better than my students. I've wasted more time than I care to admit transfixed, zombie-like, by my so-called smartphone. Teens consume a jaw-dropping nine hours of media a day—more time than they spend sleeping, much less conversing with adults.

The photographer Eric Pickersgill has captured how our devices have distanced us from each other. He asks his subjects to pose in everyday positions; then he takes away their cellphones. His aptly titled *Removed* series captures people staring blankly at their vacant hands—at what he calls a kind of *phantom limb*:

> This phantom limb is used as a way of signaling busyness and unapproachability to strangers while existing as an addictive force that promotes the splitting of attention between those who are physically with you and those who are not.[1]

The photographs are chilling, void. A family gathered around a dinner table gazes at their palms. Two friends on a park bench,

---

[1] "Removed: Project Statement": http://www.ericpickersgill.com/removed/.

both slouching into their cupped hands. An auditorium full of people, all entranced by their own empty fingers. A couple in bed, backs turned to each other. By removing the devices, he revealed our omnipresent self-absenting. The fixation would be almost transcendent, if the object weren't so banal. *Tell me to what you pay attention and I will tell you who you are.*[2]

Attention! We have it, we hold it, we pay it. Too often these days, our concentrated consciousness is taken, fractured by the merchants of distraction, who know that information-richness produces attention-impoverishment. We give away one of our most priceless resources, even though *hardly any faculty is more important for the intellectual progress of man than the power of Attention.*[3]

Worse, our devices demand a peculiar kind of *complicity* from us. We grow to share their assumptions about *what's* worth attending to.

The root of *attention* means to *stretch toward* something. It's both a physical and a mental effort—one yearns to become one with the object, *the slender tendrils of the mind* curling around it.[4] We *attend* to it, just as a servant must attend to a ruler—with all the docility and contortion that implies. When Shakespeare speaks of a character *here attend[ing] you*, it doesn't mean being merely present, but something more akin to readiness for command; an expectant waiting; intensive listening. *Minding.* The opposite is when *your mind is tossing on the ocean*[5]—your mind's there, not here.

Our devices take advantage of deep human biases: to notice the novel, the threatening, the enticing. While I find my students ever more distractible, I'm sure that my own teachers said the same of my cohort, and theirs before them, as in 1917: *The youth of today*

---

[2] José Ortega y Gasset, *Man and Crisis* (Norton, 1962), 94.

[3] Charles Darwin, *The Descent of Man, and Selection in Relation to Sex* (1971; Princeton University Press, 1981), 44.

[4] Francis Bacon, *New Organon*, in *The Works of Francis Bacon*, vol. 4, ed. James Spedding, Robert Leslie Ellis, and Douglas Denon Hearth (Cambridge University Press, 2011), 246.

[5] *Much Ado About Nothing* (5.4.36). *The Merchant of Venice* (1.1.8).

[have their] attention scattered and diverted over a wide area of interests.[6] More than a century before that, William Cowper bemoaned how

> Habits of close attention, thinking heads,
> Become more rare as dissipation spreads.[7]

But I don't think it discounts our current predicament to allow that others before us have been worried about *whether we gain or not by this habit of profuse communication.*[8] Here I stand with Henry David Thoreau:

> Our inventions are wont to be pretty toys, which distract our attention from serious things. They are but improved means to an unimproved end, an end which it was already but too easy to arrive at. . . . We are in great haste to construct a magnetic telegraph from Maine to Texas, but Maine and Texas, it may be, have nothing important to communicate.[9]

Georg Simmel concurred:

> It is true that we now have acetylene and electrical light instead of oil lamps; but the enthusiasm for the progress achieved in lighting makes us sometimes forget that the essential thing is not the lighting itself but what becomes more fully visible. People's ecstasy concerning the triumphs of the telegraph and telephone often makes them overlook the fact that what matters is the value of what one has to say, and that, compared with this, the speed or slowness of the means of communication is often a concern that could attain its present status only by usurpation.[10]

---

[6] *Fargo (ND) Courier-News,* October 5, 1917. My thanks to Matthew Harrison for the lead.

[7] "Retirement," in *Poems by William Cowper, of the Inner Temple, Esq.* (London, 1782).

[8] Virginia Woolf, *Jacob's Room* (1922), ed. Kate Flint (Oxford University Press, 2005), 171.

[9] *The Writings of Henry David Thoreau: Walden* (1854), ed. J. Lyndon Shanley (Princeton University Press, 1971), 52.

[10] "The Style of Life," in *The Philosophy of Money* (1900), trans. Tom Bottomore and David Frisby (Routledge, 1978), 523.

Religious, philosophical, and pedagogical traditions have devoted extraordinary resources to honing attention, to mitigate our innate tendency to *look another way*.[11] Admitting the fallibility of our attention isn't the same thing as saying it's impossible to improve it. As Epictetus admonishes us, *You become what you give your attention to.*[12]

Four centuries ago, John Donne preached about our divided selves, starting with his own distracted presence:

> I am not all here, I am here now preaching upon this text, and I am at home in my library considering whether Saint Gregory, or Saint Jerome, have said best of this text, before. I am here speaking to you, and yet I consider by the way, in the same instant, what it is likely you will say to one another when I have done.[13]

He's already anticipating how the audience will evaluate his words afterward. Anyone who's ever sweated through a speech is familiar with this split consciousness. You're there, you're speaking, but you're also not *there* . . . thinking instead about what you didn't do to prepare, and worrying about what the audience will think of what you said.

Turning to his congregation, Donne continues, wryly, *You are not all here neither; you are here now, hearing me, and yet you are thinking that you have heard a better sermon somewhere else, of this text before . . .*

Yup, guilty as charged. (This might be the only time I've heard a speaker admit this.) The mind wanders even further in Donne's fable:

> You are here, and you remember [to] your selves that now you think of it: This had been the fittest time, now, when every body else is at Church, to have made such and such a private visit; and because you would be there, you are there.

[11] Sonnet 7, line12.
[12] *Art of Living*, trans. Sharon Lobell (HarperOne, 2007), 52.
[13] Funeral sermon for Sir William Cokayne, December 12, 1626, in *Donne's Sermons*, ed. Logan Pearsall Smith (Oxford University Press, 1920), 3–4.

And there *we* are.

My high school librarian, Louis Jenkins, also composed prose poems (some of which later became the play *Nice Fish*, in collaboration with Shakespearean actor Mark Rylance). His elliptical paragraphs often pivot around some everyday cliché, which when held up to light becomes prismatic. His poem "Here and There" reads like an updating of Donne's sermon:

> Some days I don't know if I'm coming or going, as they say. Don't know if I'm here or there. I am here and you are there. Except, of course, when you are here or I am there. I much prefer it when you are here. Then it seems that spring is truly on the way, that the sun is warming and the lilacs will bloom. But then sometimes I think that you are not really here, that there is a faraway look in your eyes, that in fact you are far away. I don't know where you are, London? New York? Maybe you are just outside the door, but you are there and I am still here.

By dramatizing our errant minds, Donne and Jenkins arrest our attention, enacting *a momentary stay against confusion.*[14]

Shakespeare's era was vexed by the disintegrating nature of distraction. They figured it as a kind of self-forgetfulness, even madness. Recall the Folio's haunting stage direction: *Enter Ophelia, distracted* (4.2). This follows a half dozen other variations on *distraction*, most notably Hamlet's reference to his memory in *this distracted globe* (1.5.97). He's pointing literally to his own confused head, but obliquely to the Globe Theatre and its audience, and perhaps even more broadly to the entire, confounded world. *This distracted globe* still makes for a grimly accurate subtitle for our own era!

Distraction means loss of alignment. In contrast, attention recovers alignment, as in Thomas More's 1533 account of a formerly

---

[14] Louis Jenkins, "Here and There," in *In the Sun Out of the Wind*, Will o' the Wisp Books, Copyright © 2017. Reprinted with permission of the author. Robert Frost, "The Figure a Poem Makes" (1939), *The Collected Prose of Robert Frost*, edited by Mark Richardson (Harvard University Press, 2010), 132.

mad man: *He gathered hys remembraunce to hym and began to come agayne to hym selfe.*[15] Reading something together can help us *stand still*, as one of Donne's poems commands: hold your attention here, now, even though such attention is fleeting.[16] Think of King Lear's plea to a dying Cordelia: *stay a little* (5.3.245). Frank Bruni recalls his professor Anne Hall *swooning and swaying* as she recited Lear's words:

> it wasn't just her voice that trembled. It was all of her.... "Stay a little." She showed how that simple request harbored such grand anguish, capturing a fallen king's hunger for connection and his tenuous hold on sanity and contentment. And thus she taught us how much weight a few syllables can carry, how powerful the muscle of language can be. She demonstrated the rewards of close attention. And the way she did this—her eyes wild with fervor, her body aquiver with delight—was an encouragement of passion and a validation of the pleasure to be wrung from art.... Was this a luxury? Sure. But it was also the steppingstone to a more aware, thoughtful existence. College was the quarry where I found it.[17]

We can become more present to each other by sharing a common object for our focus. People attend together, *side by side; their eyes look ahead;*[18] they

> wear the same rapt expression,
> forgetting themselves in a function.
>
> How beautiful it is,
> that eye-on-the-object look.[19]

---

[15] "Apology" (1533), in *The Complete Works of Sir Thomas More*, vol. 9, ed. J. B. Trapp (Yale University Press, 1979), 118.

[16] "A Lecture upon the Shadow," in *The Songs and Sonets of John Donne*, ed. Theodore Redpath (Harvard University Press, 2009).

[17] "College's Priceless Value," *New York Times*, February 11, 2015.

[18] C. S. Lewis, *The Four Loves* (Harcourt Brace Jovanovich, 1960), 98.

[19] W. H. Auden, "Sext," *Horae Canonicae* (1954), in *Collected Shorter Poems 1927–1957* (Faber and Faber, 1966), 325.

It is just this *contact with things . . . which is precisely the beginning of knowledge. Let knowledge be the mark.*[20]

As children gaze into their own idiosyncratic devices, in a digital perversion of "personalized learning," I worry that education has given up on any kind of common object, even within a single class. The enduring power of dramatic performance, even in the face of endless distractions, confirms that there's something peculiar about sharing something together. We ought to think of the studio, the classroom, the theater as focal points for practiced attention—perhaps even a rehearsal space for democracy.[21]

Iris Murdoch asked, *What should be taught in schools?* Her answer's as simple as it's daunting: *To attend . . . to learn to desire to learn.*[22] Murdoch borrowed her concept of attention from Simone Weil, who held that while school exercises *only develop a lower kind of attention*, such exercises still cultivate the ground for higher forms. For this reason, *the development of the faculty of attention forms the real object and almost the sole interest of studies.*[23] Weil went so far as to assert that *attention, taken to its highest degree, is the same thing as prayer. . . . Absolutely unmixed attention is prayer.*[24] In this sentiment, she echoes seventeenth-century thinker Nicolas Malebranche: *Attention is the natural prayer that we make to inward truth.*[25]

One need not be religious to concur that lending our *best attention* is as rare as it's desirable.[26]

---

[20] Cornelis Verhoeven, *The Philosophy of Wonder*, trans. Mary Foran (Macmillan, 1972), 17. Sonnet 5, line 7, *The Passionate Pilgrim*.

[21] A claim made by Richard Sennett in "The Pnyx and the Agora," in *Designing Politics: The Limits of Design*, ed. Adam Kaasa, John Bingham-Hall, and Elisabetta Pietrostefani (Theatrum Mundi, 2016): http://eprints.lse.ac.uk/68075/1/Designing-Politics-The-limits-of-design.pdf.

[22] *Metaphysics as a Guide to Morals* (Penguin Books, 1992), 179.

[23] "Reflections on the Right Use of School" (1942), in *Waiting on God* (Routledge, 2009), 32.

[24] *Simone Weil: An Anthology*, ed. Siân Miles (Grove Press, 2000), 212.

[25] Cited in David Marno, *Death Be Not Proud* (University of Chicago Press, 2016), 1.

[26] *Cymbeline* (5.5.117).

Rembrandt, *Christ and the Adulteress* (c. 1650). Nationalmuseum Stockholm (Photo: Hans Thorwid).

7

OF TECHNOLOGY

"The Thinker"

Holding his chin
thinking
how to
hold the chin
and watch the computer
do
the thinking.
—William Marr, *Autumn
Window* (1996)[1]

Jorge Luis Borges crafted fables that crystallized our own technological quandaries. In one such story, a Bible salesman appears at
the narrator's door, offering a fantastic book

> called the Book of Sand because neither the book nor sand has a
> beginning or an end. . . . The number of pages in this book is liter-
> ally infinite. No page is the first; none the last.

Beguiled, the narrator, purchases this "impossible book." But he
comes to find its infinitude *monstrous*, something that overwhelms
him: *I felt it was a nightmare thing, an obscene thing, and that it
defiled and corrupted reality.*

[1] "The Thinker." Copyright © 1996 by William Marr. All rights reserved. Selected Poems
from *Autumn Window*, Arbor Hill Press.

Desperate to be rid of this diabolical volume, he hides the book in the National Library. Borges's "Book of Sand"[2] resonates with a larger problem at the heart of technology: the problem of infinity, so to speak. The problem of being overwhelmed, lost. The problem of wasting time without guidance. There's something about sand that lends itself to infinity, just as there's something about the computer.

Our era's recurrent fable? Presuming that the *only* kind of technology is *digital* technology—and that digital technology improves upon anything that preceded it. This fable amounts to a creed, unshakable in the face of mounting evidence that computers *don't* improve learning.[3] Instead, they exacerbate (not mitigate) inequality, and may even degrade the precise habits that education ought to cultivate. When confronted by dismal results, the *technological bluff*[4] is always *The next version will be better!*

Being skeptical about the forces promoting techno-utopianism doesn't make you *against* technology. (The original Luddites wanted machines that made high-quality goods, run by trained workers who were compensated fairly.)[5] But naive enthusiasm for digital technology often derives from an unspoken hostility toward teachers—a hostility that seeks to eliminate the human element from education by automating it. Sometimes such hostility gets expressed overtly:

> We've got the internet—you have so much information available. Why do you have to keep paying different lecturers to teach the same course? You get one solid lecturer and put it up online

---

[2] Trans. Andrew Hurley, *The Book of Sand and Shakespeare's Memory* (Penguin, 1998).

[3] Sean Coughlan, "Computers 'Do Not Improve' Pupil Results, Says OECD," *BBC*, September 15, 2015: http://www.bbc.com/news/business-34174796.

[4] Jacques Ellul, *The Technological Bluff* (W. B. Eerdmans, 1990). In the 1992 documentary *The Betrayal by Technology*, Ellul rebuked the illusion that
  if you just use enough technical aids you will be freer . . . "Free to do what?"

[5] Clive Thompson, "When Robots Take All of Our Jobs, Remember the Luddites," *Smithsonian Magazine*, January 2017.

and have everybody available to that knowledge for a whole lot cheaper?[6]

Ours is an age which is proud of machines that think, and suspicious of any man who tries to.[7]

Carter G. Woodson was right: *The mere imparting of information is not education.*[8] If people were content with just "content delivery," libraries and textbooks would have made schools defunct. People (and institutions) help guide us (and chide us) to confront demanding material.

Teachers have always employed "technology"—including the book, one of the most flexible and dynamic learning technologies ever created. But it's technology in the guiding hands of the learned teacher that helps situate us toward an end, not the nightmarish "Book of Sand" that has no beginning and no end. Too often we mistake the instrument for a method.

When we are using computers, we are already thinking with sand: the glass on our screens is derived from sand, as is *the miniaturized writing in the sand that links thousands of transistors on a silicon chip.*[9] Indeed, sand has been a material substrate for thought for millennia. It's been speculated that the Hindu-Arabic numeral system derived from sand-scripted origins. Sand tables have long been part of pedagogy, whether in ancient Greek mathematics or in eighteenth-century Indian literacy instruction.[10]

[6] Senator Ron Johnson of Wisconsin, cited by Scott Jaschik, "Ken Burns or Instructors?" *Inside Higher Ed*, August 22, 2016.

[7] Howard Mumford Jones, cited in *Technocracy Digest*, August 1951, 5. Nicholas Negroponte looks forward to the day you can "swallow a pill and know Shakespeare." *I have no words. (Macbeth* 5.7.37). https://blog.ted.com/back-to-techs-future-nicholas-negroponte-at-ted2014/.

[8] *The Mis-Education of the Negro* (Associated Publishers, 1933), ix.

[9] Joseph Tabbi, "Democratic Politics in the Virtual Classroom," in *Internet Culture*, ed. David Porter (Routledge 1997), 243.

[10] Patricia Crain, "Children of Media, Children as Media: Optical Telegraphs, Indian Pupils, and Joseph Lancaster's System for Cultural Reproduction," in *New Media 1740–1915*, ed. Lisa Gitelman and Geoffrey B. Pingree (MIT Press, 2004), 72.

Metal type was cast in sand as early as the fourteenth century in China and Korea.

Sand plays a pivotal role in Shakespeare's *Titus Andronicus*, permitting the violated Lavinia to reveal the names of her rapists by transcribing them in a *sandy plot* (4.1.69). In his era, sand was sprinkled onto manuscripts to blot wet ink, speeding up the drying process. One Enlightenment writer went so far as to analogize the mind itself to a sandy imprint:

> The human brain is a bodily substance; and sensible and permanent impressions made upon it must so far resemble those made on sand by the foot . . . as to have certain shape, length, breadth, and deepness.[11]

Now, I'm not saying that every classroom should be outfitted with sandboxes. Nor do I think that taking students to the beach will solve all our math problems! But thinking with sand can help us reflect on how thought itself is *techne*—the art of fitting things together, as a carpenter, or joiner.[12]

Eubulides, a pupil of a pupil of Socrates, deployed sand to consider how we categorize things. His sorites paradox (from the Greek word meaning heaping up) asks us to imagine a heap of sand. From this pile, remove one grain. Then, remove another. Then, another. And another . . . and another . . . at what point is it no longer a heap? Are three grains a heap? Is *one*?

Shakespeare's *King Lear* plays out the sorites paradox in the accelerating reduction of Lear's retinue, whittled down by his daughters from one hundred, to fifty, then (hastily): *What need you five-and-twenty? Ten? Or five? . . . What need one?*[13] The imag-

---

[11] James Beattie, *Dissertations Moral and Critical: On Memory and Imagination* (London, 1783), 11–12.

[12] *"Techne" derives from the Indo-European root "tek," which . . . means "to fit together the woodwork of a . . . house."*
David Roochnik, *Of Art and Wisdom: Plato's Understanding of Techne* (Pennsylvania State University Press, 1996), 19.

[13] *King Lear* (2.3.256, 258).

ined sand heap is a kind of pedagogical technology, albeit an *immaterial* one: a conceptual tool, or process, designed to help us refine our thinking, by concentrating our thoughts.

When the Greek scientist Archimedes set *his* mind to thinking, reckoning how many grains of sand would fill the universe inspired him to invent the concept of what we would now call exponents. Archimedes serves as a cautionary figure for us as well, since it was his absorption in drawing figures in the sand that led him to ignore an invading Roman soldier, who killed him when Archimedes yelled, *Do not disturb that sand!* (This anecdote of intellectual devotion would later inspire Sophie Germain, the French mathematician who investigated Fermat's Last Theorem.)

Following Archimedes, Christopher Clavius would in 1607 calculate an even more precise estimate of *the number of grains of sand which would be required to fill the whole space between the earth and the stars.*[14] John Donne, taken with Clavius's inconceivably large number, cited it in his sermons as a way to convey the unimaginable scope of the Divine:

> But if the whole space to the firmament were filled with sand, and we had before us Clavius's number, how many thousands would be; if all that space were filled with water, and so joined the waters above with the waters below the firmament, and we had the number of all those drops of water; and then had every single sand, and every single drop multiplied by the whole number of both, we were still short of numbering the benefits of God, as God; but then, of God in Christ, infinitely, superinfinitely short.[15]

Shakespeare invokes the proverbial futility of counting sand: *The task he undertakes / Is numb'ring sands.*[16] *Edward III*, a play some

[14] John Carey, *John Donne: Life, Mind, and Art* (Oxford University Press, 1981), 134.
[15] Sermon LXXV, Preached to the King at Whitehall, April 15, 1628.
[16] *Richard II* (2.2.145–46).

recent scholars have attributed at least in part to Shakespeare, has a similar passage:

> As many sands as these my hands can hold
> Are but my handful of so many sands.
> Then, all the world's—and call it but a power—
> Easily ta'en up and quickly thrown away;
> But if I stand to count them sand by sand,
> The number would confound my memory
> And make a thousand millions of a task
> Which, briefly, is no more indeed than one.[17]

Donne thought with sand in a more mundane manner, yet one that endures as a fundamental technology of classrooms: the technology of "keeping time." In yet another self-reflexive sermon,

> [Donne] punctuates his point by drawing attention to the [standard pulpit] hourglass that has been marking the passage of time during the course of his preaching and informing his congregation that he is out of time: "But we are now in the work of an houre, and no more. If there be a minute of sand left, (There is not)."[18]

The unit of the class hour (or fifty minutes, or seventy-five minutes, or thirty) is arbitrary, to be sure. This has made it an easy target for mockery by those who consider it an antiquated or even oppressive residue of autocratic managerialism, to be overcome by the asynchronic space of online platforms. Yet the technology of shared time endures as a productive mutual pause—*to sit awhile and think*.[19]

And here again I am thinking of sand, through a meditation

---

[17] *Edward III* (4.4.42–49).

[18] Chapel Royal on February 11, 1627; quoting John N. Wall, "Transforming the Object of Our Study: The Early Modern Sermon and the Virtual Paul's Cross Project," *Journal of Digital Humanities* 3, no. 1 (Spring 2014).

[19] Lorraine Hansberry, *A Raisin in the Sun* (1959; Vintage, 2011), 119.

by Seamus Heaney on the limits of poetry. Heaney confessed that poems *are practically useless* in the face of *the brutality of the historical onslaught.* Yet then he counters himself, asserting that while

> in one sense the efficacy of poetry is nil—no lyric has ever stopped a tank . . . [yet, in] another sense, it is unlimited. It is like the writing in the sand in the face of which accusers and accused are left speechless and renewed.[20]

Heaney alludes to the Gospel of John, where Jesus was asked to judge whether a woman accused of adultery should be stoned. Instead of responding,

> Jesus stooped down, and with his finger wrote on the ground. And while they continued asking him, he lifted himself up, and said unto them, "Let him that is among you without sin, cast the first stone at her." And again he stooped down, and wrote on the ground. And when they heard it, being accused by their own conscience, they went out one by one, beginning at the eldest even to the last.

Heaney concludes:

> The drawing of those [unknown] characters [in the sand] is like poetry, a break with the usual life but not an absconding from it. Poetry, like the writing [in the sand], is arbitrary and marks time in every possible sense of that phrase [*marks time*]. It does not say to the accusing crowd or the helpless accused, 'Now a solution will take place,' it does not propose to be instrumental or effective. Instead, in the rift between what is going to happen and whatever we would wish to happen, poetry holds attention for a space, functions not as distraction but as pure concentration, a focus where our power to concentrate is concentrated back on ourselves.

[20] *The Government of the Tongue* (Farrar, Straus and Giroux, 1990), 107–8.

This *marking collective time* likewise characterizes the classroom, itself both a temporal and a spatial technology.

One last instance of thinking with sand, from the Socratic dialogue *Meno*. Socrates, as usual, has reached an impasse with his interlocutor and turns to Meno's slave to consider the geometrical problem of doubling the area of a square. This scene dramatizes one of the first instances of teaching and technology, a scene as memorable for its limits as for its successes.

The writing in the sand is *instrumental*, the means to an end. It would be a gross error to mistake the technology for the end itself.

The writing in the sand is *ad hoc*, done for *this* person, and *this* moment in time; the technological strategy *arises* in response to the occasion, rather than being forced upon the scenario from the outside.

The writing in the sand provides a *focal point*, as an object for collective thought. But we must, must remember that the technology is *not* the thought itself.

And the writing in the sand is *temporary*, *disposable* when it no longer serves its purpose.

I was recently invited to speak—as the token nonscientist—on a faculty panel about teaching and technology. Afraid I was being asked to play the straw-man (maybe sand-man!) opponent of their tech-savvy triumphs, I prepared as my lifeline a PowerPoint presentation, stacked with slides about Borges, silicon chips, the Hindu-Arabic numeral system, Indian sand tables, Korean type casting, the sorites paradox, Archimedes's reckoner, portraits of Germain and Cavius, Donne's hourglass, Rembrandt's drawing, Platonic geometry. All this, and more, for my allotted five minutes.

Then, *pat!* it came, *like the catastrophe of the old comedy*.[21] The projector refused to work, no matter how we coaxed it. My lifeline

---

[21] *King Lear* (1.2.123).

had proved to be a *rope of sands*.[22] Thankfully, my handout didn't require a new bulb or software update.

When I finally stated my power-less point, I was heartened to find common cause with my colleagues from Physics and Computer Science. They're just as concerned as I am about evaporating attention spans and device-induced zombie-ism.

It's human to avoid the hard work of thinking, reading, and writing. But we all fail when technology becomes a distraction from, or, worse, a substitute for, the interminable yet rewarding task of confronting the object under study—*see[ing] the world in a grain of sand*.[23]

---

[22] "The Collar," *George Herbert: 100 Poems*, edited by Helen Wilcox (Cambridge, 2016), 123.

[23] William Blake, *Auguries of Innocence* (c. 1803), in *William Blake: Selected Poems*, ed. Nicholas Shrimpton (Oxford University Press, 2019), 77.

Le cadet des soucis (1972), © Keystone-France/Gamma Rapho K003368_A4.

8

OF IMITATION

If you can't imitate him, don't copy him.
—Yogi Berra, *Baseball Digest* (1969)

Quick quiz: which one of these magicians' speeches was written by Shakespeare?

> 1a: *Ye elves of hills, of brooks, of woods alone, of standing lakes,*
> 1b: *Ye elves of hills, brooks, standing lakes and groves*

What the elves!?

OK, how about these lavish descriptions of Cleopatra on her barge?

> 2a: *the poop whereof was gold, the sails of purple, and the oars of silver . . . she was laid under a pavilion of cloth-of-gold of tissue*
> 2b: *the poop was beaten gold, purple the sails . . . the oars were silver . . . she did lie in her pavilion—cloth of gold, of tissue*

Poop—that's a tough one.

But these features of an ideal society must be easy to distinguish:

> 3a: *no kind of traffic, no knowledge of letters . . . no name of magistrate . . . no use of service . . . no contracts, no successions . . . no occupation but idle . . . no use of wine, corn, or metal*
> 3b: *no kind of traffic . . . no name of magistrate; letters should not be known . . . use of service, none; contract, succession . . . none; no use of metal, corn, or wine . . . no occupation; all men idle*

(The answers are all "b." If you responded "not 2b," you get credit for being a witty fool.)

Shakespeare's versions are almost indistinguishable from his sources.[1] I confess I've massaged his verse to read more like the prose of 2a and 3a, as well as regularized spelling and capitalization, which was erratic in this period: *To learne to wrytte doune Ingglisshe wourdes in Chaxper's daie was notte dificulte.*[2]

My students are anxious about charges of plagiarism in their own writing. So whenever I present them with these paired passages, they scoff: *What a rip-off!* (That, or they adopt T. S. Eliot's dictum *Immature poets imitate; mature poets steal.*)[3] Someone caught with this kind of unattributed borrowing today could face failure, or even expulsion.

Now, to be fair, Shakespeare's borrowing—from poems, proverbs, romances, legal cases, biblical passages, popular ballads, short stories, historical chronicles, contemporary events, classical mythology, or lots and lots of plays (whether for *tragedy, comedy, history, pastoral, pastoral-comical, historical-pastoral, tragical-historical, tragical-comical-historical-pastoral*)[4]—tends to be diffuse, far less direct than these culled examples.

But the overall point holds: the entire era preceding the nineteenth century had a different sense of what counted as "originality," and what counted as "plagiarism." As someone once said, of making many books there is no end:

---

[1] 1a. Arthur Golding's 1567 translation of Ovid's *Metamorphoses* (7.265–66).

1b. *The Tempest* (5.1.33).

2a. Sir Thomas North's 1579 translation of Plutarch's *Lives of the noble Grecians and Romans.*

2b. *Antony and Cleopatra* (2.2.204–11).

3a. John Florio's 1603 translation of Michel de Montaigne's "Of Cannibals."

3b. *The Tempest* (2.1.143–49).

[2] Anthony Burgess, *Shakespeare* (Knopf, 1970), 29.

[3] Discussing Shakespeare's contemporary Philip Massinger in *The Sacred Wood* (Knopf, 1921), 114.

[4] *Hamlet* (2.2.324–26).

Laurence Sterne, *Tristram Shandy* (1761): *Shall we for ever make new books, as apothecaries make new mixtures, by pouring only out of one vessel into another? Are we for ever to be twisting and untwisting the same rope?*

Robert Burton, preface to *The Anatomy of Melancholy* (1621): *As apothecaries, we make new mixtures every day, pour out of one vessel into another... We weave the same web still, twist the same rope again and again.*

Thomas Cooper's Tudor dictionary copies the definition of "plagiary" without citing his source—as his definition in turn would be copied by his peers!

Plagiarism isn't even the right word, since modern legal copyright didn't exist until 1710. Before then, being "original" meant wrestling with your predecessors, your "authors," your sources of authority. You even called them your "originals" (as Milton said of Spenser) as you made "creative imitations," a phrase that unsettles yet reconciles its (only apparent) contradiction in its terms.

This is the opposite of how we now conceive of "creativity" in today's schooling. "Imitation" sounds pejorative to us: a fake, a knockoff, a mere copy; at best, derivative drudge work. As a result, there's an indifference to the still-valid practices of emulation (and repetition, and memorization), which are purported to quash independent thought.

This is a loss. If anything, *creative imitation*—a dynamic intermingling of reflection and practice, thinking and doing—has been the hallmark of art and industry since one *Homo faber* copied the chip off another's block. We think *through* inherited forms, because *we are a world of imitations*, as Virginia Woolf marveled.[5] It's

---

[5] August 12, 1899, in *Passionate Apprentice: The Early Journals, 1897–1909* (Random House, 2018), 227.

bizarre that people think they could learn to write without engaging with other writers. Gary Snyder had no patience for poets

> not being willing to read books, for Christ's sake. You run into people who want to write poetry who don't want to read anything in the tradition. That's like wanting to be a builder but not finding out what different kinds of wood you use.[6]

Snyder's carpentry conceit is sustained by Eleanor Catton, the youngest-ever winner of the Booker Prize:

> I believe really strongly in imitation, actually: I think it's the first place you need to go to if you're going to be able to understand how something works. True mimicry is actually quite difficult. . . . You want to enlarge your toolbox, and enlarge what is available to you as a writer.[7]

Derek Walcott concurs:

> How does a poet teach himself or herself? I think chiefly by imitation, chiefly by practising it as a deliberate technical exercise often. Translation, imitation, those were my methods anyway.[8]

Think of Elizabeth Bishop, absorbing Robert Lowell, Marianne Moore, Gerard Manley Hopkins, Felicia Hemans, Alfred Tennyson, Charles Baudelaire, William Wordsworth, William Blake, Daniel Defoe, George Herbert, Philip Sidney, the Bible. If, per Voltaire, *originality is nothing but judicious imitation*, then Bertolt Brecht (himself a shrewd rewriter of Shakespeare) was right: *Anyone can be creative, it's rewriting other people that's a challenge.*[9]

While the brash proclamations of the 1841 Ralph Waldo Em-

[6] "The Real Work," *Ohio Review* 18, no. 3 (1977): 67–105.

[7] Anthony Jenkins, interview, *Globe and Mail*, March 25, 2017.

[8] Simon Stanford, interview with Derek Walcott (April 28, 2005): https://www.nobel prize.org/prizes/literature/1992/walcott/25106-interview-transcript-1992/.

[9] "Anecdotes of Voltaire," *The Lady's Magazine* 17 (1786): 378; Eric Bentley, *Bentley on Brecht*, 3rd ed. (Northwestern University Press, 2008), 390.

erson enthrall us (*never imitate*; *imitation is suicide*), the mature Emerson in 1876 yielded that

> the debt is immense to past thought. None escapes it. The originals are not original. There is imitation, model, and suggestion, to the very archangels, if we knew their history.[10]

If we knew their history—we keep forgetting that history, as it keeps slipping away from us. As Dryden remarked: *The poet who borrows nothing from others is yet to be born. Is Versailles the less a new building, because the architect of that palace hath imitated others which were built before it?*[11]

Even the most extreme form of imitation—raw reproduction—generates insight. A teenage Judd Apatow transcribed verbatim dialogue from taped episodes of *Saturday Night Live*, working out the most important element of comedy (*TIMING!*). James Wright typed out Rilke's German sonnets, *to better hear their music*;[12] Hunter S. Thompson did the same with Fitzgerald, Hemingway, and Faulkner, *to feel what it feels like to write that well*.[13] Abraham Lincoln knew *Aesop's Fables* so intimately *that he could rewrite it from memory without the loss of a single word; [he would] copy passages from model writers in much the same manner*.[14] Gwendolyn Brooks imitated Eliot, who imitated Pope, who imitated Milton, who imitated Spenser, who imitated Chaucer, who imitated Dante, who imitated Virgil, who imitated Homer, who consolidated centuries of oral transmission. Your

---

[10] "Self-Reliance," in *Essays: First Series* (J. Munroe and Company, 1841); "Quotation and Originality," in *Letters and Social Aims* (James R. Osgood, 1876).

[11] Dedication to the *Aeneid* (1697), 32.

[12] Jonathan Blunk, *James Wright: A Life in Poetry* (Farrar, Straus and Giroux, 2017), 47.

[13] Interview with Hunter S. Thompson in the documentary *Buy the Ticket, Take the Ride* (2006).

[14] Marshall Myers, "'Rugged Grandeur': A Study of the Influences on the Writing Style of Abraham Lincoln and a Brief Study of His Writing Habits," *Rhetoric Review* 23, no. 4 (2004): 350–67.

whole vocation should move beyond *endless imitation*[15]—but you still begin with imitation.

Whenever Robert Louis Stevenson read something he liked, he sat down

> and set myself to ape that quality. . . . That, like it or not, is the way to learn to write . . . it was so, if we could trace it out, that all men have learned . . . Shakespeare himself, the imperial, proceeds directly from a school. It is only from a school that we can expect to have good writers. . . . Before he can tell what cadences he truly prefers, the student should have tried all that are possible; before he can choose and preserve a fitting key of words, he should long have practised the literary scales; and it is only after years of such gymnastic that he can sit down at last, legions of words swarming to his call, dozens of turns of phrase simultaneously bidding for his choice, and he himself knowing what he wants to do and (within the narrow limit of a man's ability) able to do it.[16]

Stevenson hits so many right notes here: the insecurity about "aping" (a long-standing anxiety in Shakespeare's era: is imitation "slavish" animal mimicry?); the need for incessant practice, as in sports or music; and the wondrous way in which, by trying to sound like someone else, you begin to sound "like yourself," with a greater command of your range—what André Malraux characterized as evolving *from pastiche to style*.[17]

Out of frustration at his youthful ineloquence, Benjamin Franklin purchased copies of the eighteenth-century periodical *The Spectator*, a model of powerful style. He *wish'd if possible to imitate it*:

---

[15] William Wordsworth, "Ode: Intimations of Immortality from Recollections of Early Childhood," lines 107–8.

[16] "Learning to Write" (1888).

[17] Cited by Harold Bloom in *The Anxiety of Influence* (1973; Oxford University Press, 1997), 26.

With that View, I took some of the Papers, & making short Hints of the Sentiment in each Sentence, laid them by a few Days, and then without looking at the Book, try'd to compleat the Papers again, by expressing each hinted Sentiment at length & as fully as it had been express'd before, in any suitable Words that should come to hand. Then I compar'd my Spectator with the Original, discover'd some of my Faults & corrected them.[18]

Even coders recommend "The Benjamin Franklin Programming Practice Model":

1 Find a program that you greatly admire and read it.
2 Take notes on the roles, inputs, and outputs of each major component.
3 Take notes on how the components interact.
4 Rewrite the program.
5 Compare your code with the original.
6 Note where you can improve and study accordingly.
   Don't just write more programs. Super charge your abilities by studying great programs, and then trying to imitate them.[19]

In copying an original, and then comparing his imitation to that original, Franklin replicated the method of Renaissance educators: *double translation*. Take a Latin model; translate it into the vernacular; now translate your version back again into Latin; now compare the original Latin source (L1) with your "double-translated" Latin (L2).

That's even tougher than it sounds! You need to figure out not only what Cicero (or Ovid or Seneca or Virgil or whoever) said; you need to figure out *how* they said it. You must catch all of the traits of their style in your own language—and then reverse the

[18] *Autobiography* (Library of America, 1990), 15.
[19] Louie Dinh, "How Benjamin Franklin Would've Learned to Program" (September 20, 2013): https://github.com/louiedinh/python-practice-projects/blob/master/content /blog/how-benjamin-franklin-learned-to-program.md.

process to sound like Cicero (or Ovid or Seneca or Virgil or whomever) in Latin again. This simple yet radical assignment provides its own correcting mechanism, as you can measure how distant L2 sounds from L1.

While the Latin curriculum has since vanished, this method still works today. I've had students translate Shakespeare's sonnets into another language (whether their first or second) and back again. I've also had them modify the opening sentences of the Declaration of Independence into modern English, then back again.[20] The effort makes you attend to the texture of texts; appreciate nuance; and close the distance across cultures and time. Ultimately, *translation is your way of learning your own language*.[21] What is the best way to say this? What's at stake?

Northrop Frye cautioned that we *tend to follow the structure of the language we're thinking in*. How to avoid these ruts, and make use of *our minds at full capacity*, instead of *turning on a tap and letting a lot of platitudinous bumble emerge*?

> The best check on this so far discovered is some knowledge of other languages, where at least the bumble has to fit into a different set of grammatical grooves. . . . humanists have always insisted that you don't learn to think wholly from one language: you learn to think better from linguistic conflict, from bouncing one language off another.[22]

Now, this is not to say that the ideal of imitation wasn't fraught with tension. Is one supposed to reproduce the model perfectly? (Sometimes yes; Petrarch thought no.) Can emulation be competitive? (No doubt!) Is there a risk that, per Ben Jonson, *we so insist in imitating others, as we cannot (when it is necessary) return to*

---

[20] Danielle Allen's *Our Declaration* (Norton, 2014) walks through a slow reading, made in close conjunction with her nontraditional students. It's a model of inspired, care-full thinking.

[21] Ezra Pound's advice to W. S. Merwin, cited in *The Poetry Archive*: https://www.poetry archive.org/poet/ws-merwin.

[22] *The Educated Imagination* (1963; House of Anansi Press, 2002), 72.

ourselves?[23] (Perhaps; but as long as the goal remains to move beyond imitation, I'm not so worried.) Many early modern writers expressed serious reservations about the practice—including Shakespeare, albeit through the voice of a pedant: *Imitari is nothing: so doth the hound his master, the ape his keeper, the tired horse his rider.*[24]

Yet Aristotle goes so far as to call us *most imitative of living creatures.*[25] If William James was right that *each of us is in fact what he is almost exclusively by virtue of his imitativeness,*[26] then we must think hard about what and how we imitate. As James Baldwin cautioned, *children have never been very good at listening to their elders, but they have never failed to imitate them. They must, they have no other models.*[27]

Imitation has beneficial consequences; as Addison (himself the model for Franklin) affirmed with gratitude, *in imitating such great Authors I have always excelled myself.*[28] All education comprises subject formation, so you might as well craft a sequence of learning that best takes advantage of our tendencies, rather than ignoring them.

Christopher Simpson advised aspiring baroque composers to take the score of *some of the best esteemed Composers in that kind of Musick*, place a blank score beneath it, and *prick them down*—that is, use a needle to puncture the paper in order to create *a Pattern to imitate.*[29] Like Hunter S. Thompson's physical attempt to *feel what it feels like* to write well, this patterning places the apprentice

---

[23] *Timber, or Discoveries* (1640–41), in *The Complete Poems*, ed. George Parfitt (Penguin, 1996), 407.

[24] *Love's Labor's Lost* (4.2.118–19).

[25] *Poetics* (4.2) (c. 350 BCE), trans. S. H. Butcher (Dover, 1951), 15.

[26] *Talks to Teachers* (Henry Holt, 1914), 48.

[27] "Fifth Avenue, Uptown: A Letter from Harlem," in *Nobody Knows My Name* (1960; Vintage, 2013), 48.

[28] *The Works of The Right Honourable Joseph Addison, Esq; In Four Volumes: Volume The Fourth* (1721), 237.

[29] *Compendium of Practical Musick* (1677), 145.

composer in the position of the master composer, reproducing her motions.

When my own students are studying a poem, I make them copy it by hand. Pause along the way, as if you were composing the words yourself. You *in-habit* your source, gaining *not a perfunctory knowledge, but an intimate familiarity with the original . . . we are, so to speak, transformed into the author's very self.*[30]

For almost two thousand years, creative imitation was omnipresent, embracing *not only literature but pedagogy, grammar, rhetoric, aesthetics, the visual arts, music, historiography, politics, and philosophy.*[31] In his chapter devoted to imitation, Quintilian speculates on why it works so well:

> It is a universal rule of life that we should wish to copy what we approve in others. . . . the elementary study of every branch of learning is directed by reference to some definite standard that is placed before the learner. We must, in fact, either be like or unlike those who have proved their excellence.[32]

Imitating good models strengthens every human endeavor, from infant sensorimotor development to the grueling practice of Olympic athletes. And, after a period of disciplined imitation, something remarkable happens. George Saunders recounts this imperceptible transition:

> Then one day—maybe age has something to do with it, or something difficult happens that brings him to a boil—he snaps. No more imitation. That's it. Something breaks. He starts sounding . . . like himself. Or at least he doesn't sound like anyone else, exactly. . . . The work he does there is not the work of his masters.

[30] Giambattista Vico, *On the Study Methods of Our Time* (1708–9), trans. Elio Gianturco (Cornell University Press, 1990), 73.

[31] Thomas Greene, *The Light in Troy* (Yale University Press, 1982), 1.

[32] *The Institutio Oratoria of Quintilian*, vol. 4, trans. H. E. Butler (G. P. Putnam's Sons, 1922), 10.2.2–3, p. 75.

It is less. It is more modest; it is messier. It is small and minor. But at least it's his.[33]

When I read Shakespeare's early plays, I get the feeling of an ambitious writer striving, through competitive imitation, to out-twin Plautus, to out-blood Seneca, to out-bombast Marlowe, to out-history Holinshed. At a certain point, he starts sounding . . . *more himself—or more than himself.*[34] As we all seek to do.

[33] "Author's Note" to *CivilWarLand in Bad Decline* (Random House, 2012), 197.
[34] Theodore Roethke, "How to Write like Somebody Else," in *On Poetry and Craft: Selected Prose* (1959; Copper Canyon Press, 2001), 62.

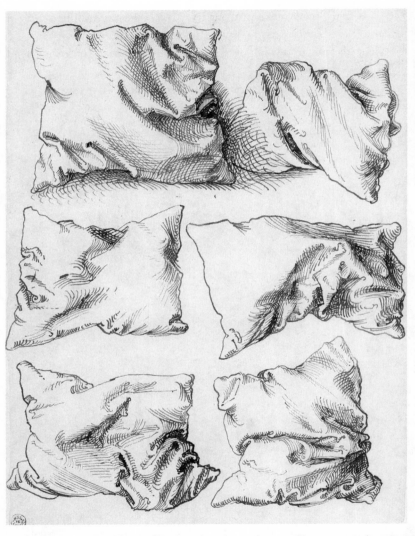

Albrecht Dürer, *Six Studies of Pillows* (1493). Robert Lehman Collection, 1975 (1975.1.862). Image copyright © The Metropolitan Museum of Art. Image source: Art Resource, NY.

9
OF EXERCISES

The intellect is a muscle; it must be exercised.
—Ta-Nehisi Coates, "How to Be a Political-Opinion Journalist" (2013)

My college track coach was named Will Freeman—now there's a Shakespearean moniker (*the fit and apt construction of thy name . . . doth import so much*)[1]! For warm-ups, Will made us stumble through *plyometrics*. After stretching, we'd have to sprint in all kinds of funny ways: backward; skipping; hopping; sidestepping scissor-like—anything but straight forward running. The textbook assigned during Shakespeare's childhood recommends writing *every waye forewarde, backwarde*[2]—a kind of verbal plyometrics.

Goofy as plyometrics felt, the goal was simple: if you want to run fast in a straight line, it helps to practice running *not* in a straight line. We were working different muscle groups, so that when we returned to our default gait, we were not only stronger, but more at ease within ourselves. This was a kind of cross-training within running, but we also did cross-training in other sports, just as football players bike, bikers swim, and swimmers drink (well, at least they did at Grinnell).

Chemistry Nobel laureate (and fellow Grinnellian) Thomas Cech makes the "cross-training" analogy between body and mind:

> The cross-training may exercise key muscle groups more effectively than spending the same amount of time working out in the

---

[1] *Cymbeline* (5.4.442–43).

[2] William Lily's *A Shorte Introduction of Grammar* (1549), cited in Jeff Dolven, *Scenes of Instruction* (University of Chicago Press, 2007), 35.

sport of interest. . . . academic cross-training develops a student's ability to collect and organize facts and opinions, to analyze them and weigh their value, and to articulate an argument, and it may develop these skills more effectively than writing yet another lab report.[3]

Just as the worst way to hit the target is to aim at the target, *in order to be an engineer, it is not enough to be an engineer.*[4] And in order to be free, being given *precisely choreographed moves to perform* is, counterintuitively, *a more successful incentive to freedom.*[5]

If *exercise both strengthens and sharpens our mind,*[6] what are the conditions for this kind of brain training? How can you get the bullies to stop kicking sand in your cerebellum?

You exercise your mind at the gym—in the *Progymnasmata*, a regimen of mental gymnastics. This was a fourteen-step rhetorical plan, which proceeded in sequenced complexity, from retelling Aesopian fables to arguing for or against a legislative proposal. Compiled in the first century CE, elaborated by Aphthonius in the fourth century, translated into Latin in the early sixteenth century (even humanist schoolmasters had trouble with Greek!), and paraphrased into English in 1563 by Richard Rainolde (an edition brought by colonists to New England), *Progymnasmata* was an enduring handbook for rhetorical study for nearly two millennia.

Rainolde's translation had the architectonic title *The FOUNDA-TION of Rhetorike*. It was a comprehensive system that forced students to imitate models; expand as well as contract narratives; become familiar with genres and media; internalize a magnificent array of formulas; compose with vivacity; rehearse disputation—

---

[3] "Science at Liberal Arts Colleges: A Better Education?" in *Distinctively American: The Residential Liberal Arts Colleges,* ed. Steven Koblik and Stephen R. Graubard (Routledge, 2000), 210.

[4] José Ortega y Gasset, "Man the Technician," in *Toward a Philosophy of History* (Norton, 1941), 103.

[5] Martha Nussbaum, recounting Rabindranath Tagore's radical pedagogy for women's equality, in *Not for Profit* (Princeton University Press, 2011), 105.

[6] John of Salisbury, citing Bernard of Chartres's pedagogy, in *Metalogican* (1169).

overall, hone their style. It was ambitious, but it provided students the infrastructure to achieve those ambitions—what Winston Churchill termed *the scaffolding of rhetoric*.[7]

As the old joke goes, how do you get to Carnegie Hall? *Practice, practice, practice.* (That's *epizeuxis*, or what Puttenham termed "Cuckoo spell": *repetition, repetition, repetition*.)[8] While students were drilled in imitation, they were also practicing by making their own compositions. This was not just "writing *across* the curriculum"; this was writing *as* the curriculum.

They practiced language in the same way a lawyer practices law, or a doctor practices medicine: all the time, as part of their active identity. This was verbal training for careers, whether in the church, the court, or the market. As Twyla Tharp believes about dance, *The routine is as much a part of the creative process as the lightning bolt of inspiration, maybe more.*[9]

The end of all these exercises was fluent *performance. It takes a great deal of experience to become natural,* Willa Cather knew.[10] Practice habituates you to "act natural." And these rhetorical habits persisted in education until quite recently. The words of a nineteenth-century schoolmaster could be just as applicable to Shakespeare's era as they were to Cicero's:

> You go to a great school not for knowledge so much as for arts and habits; for the habit of attention, for the art of expression, for the art of assuming at a moment's notice a new intellectual posture, for the art of entering quickly into another person's thoughts, for the habit of submitting to censure and refutation, for the art of

---

[7] Unpublished essay (1897), printed in Randolph S. Churchill, *Winston S. Churchill: Youth, 1874–1900, Companion Volume*, pt. 2 (Houghton Mifflin, 1967), 816–21.

[8] *The Art of English Poetry: A Critical Edition*, ed. Frank Whigham and Wayne A. Rebhorn (Cornell University Press, 2007), 285. Edgar Degas: *It is essential to do the same subject over again, ten times, a hundred times. Nothing in art must seem to be chance, not even movement.* Letter to Bartholomé (Naples, January 17, 1866), cited by Eric Protter, *Painters on Painting* (Grosset & Dunlap, 1971), 27.

[9] *The Creative Habit* (Simon & Schuster, 2003), 7.

[10] Cather interviewed by Latrobe Carroll, *Bookman*, May 3, 1921. *Willa Cather in Person*, ed. L. Brent Bohlke (University of Nebraska Press, 1986), 21.

indicating assent or dissent in graduated terms, for the habit of
regarding minute points of accuracy, for the habit of working out
what is possible in a given time, for taste, for discrimination, for
mental courage and mental soberness. Above all, you go to a great
school for self-knowledge.[11]

A Shakespearean education gives us the chance to *build* these habits of mind that individuals (and cultures) need if they're to flourish. We all need practice in curiosity, intellectual agility, the deter-
mination to analyze, commitment to resourceful communication,
historically and culturally situated reflectiveness, the confidence
to embrace complexity. In short: the ambition to create something
better, in whatever field.

We practice these habits again and again, until they become *so
much a part of you that you'll never forget them*,[12] just as we train
athletes to develop a "natural" swing, or as we train musicians in
finger exercises to develop facility with their instrument—a fact
that infuriated an impatient young Hitler![13] As George Eliot's
Herr Klesmer puts it, *Genius at first is little more than a great capacity for receiving discipline.*[14]

Likewise, experience in thinking *can be won, like all experience
in doing something, only through practice, through exercises.*[15] Erasmus knew that *the secret of style* was no secret at all: *write, write, and
again write.*[16] A recent study concluded that the best predictor for
making significant collegiate gains in reading, writing, and critical

[11] William Johnson Cory, *Eton Reform* (Longman, Green, Longman and Roberts, 1861), 6–7.

[12] Jacques Pepin, *Jacques Pepin's Complete Techniques* (Black Dog & Leventhal, 2001), vii.

[13] *This stupid 'exercising the fingers' left him raging. . . . what mattered most in music [to Hitler] was inspiration, and not finger exercises.*
August Kubizek, *The Young Hitler I Knew*, trans. Geoffrey Brooks (1953; Greenhill, 2011), 78.

[14] *Daniel Deronda* (1876), ed. Graham Handley and K. M. Newton (Oxford University Press, 2014), 216.

[15] Hannah Arendt, *Between Past and Future* (1961; Penguin, 2006), 13.

[16] *Desiderius Erasmus, Concerning the Aim and Method of Education*, trans. William Harrison Woodward (Cambridge University Press, 1904), 165. *Epizeuxis* again!

thinking . . . was completing courses with demanding requirements in reading, writing, and critical thinking.[17] *Buzz, buzz*.[18]

The seventeenth-century educator John Amos Comenius knew this:

> Craftsmen do not hold their apprentices down to theories; they put them to work without delay so that they may learn to forge metal by forging, to carve by carving, to paint by painting, to leap by leaping. Therefore in schools let the pupils learn to write by writing, to speak by speaking, to sing by singing, to reason by reasoning, etc., so that schools may simply be workshops in which work is done eagerly.[19]

Epictetus knew it even earlier:

> Every habit and every faculty is confirmed and strengthened by the corresponding acts, the faculty of walking by walking, that of running by running. If you wish to have a faculty for reading, read; if for writing, write. . . . So generally if you wish to acquire a habit for anything, do the thing.[20]

Robert Southey boils it down for us: *It is by writing much* that a person *learns to write well*.[21]

Given current educational orthodoxy that *writing in this didactic way inhibits creativity and free expression*, such a rhetorically saturated curriculum seems daunting to reproduce today. There are some hopeful exceptions, such as New Dorp High School, where *all* teachers in *all* disciplines receive training in writing. They begin with *heavily scaffolded* exercises at the level of the sentence before working up to *progressive mastery through deliberate practice*—in short, the same premises that governed the *Progymnasmata*. According to a scholar who has studied the school,

---

[17] Richard Arum and Josipa Roksa, *Academically Adrift* (University of Chicago Press, 2011).

[18] *Hamlet* (2.2.321).

[19] P. Bovet, *J. Amos Comenius* (Geneva, 1943), 23.

[20] *Discourses*, trans. P. E. Matheson (Dover, 2012), 102.

[21] Jack Simmons, *Southey* (Collins, 1945), 218.

when teachers try taking instruction back to basics . . . they see big improvements in the quality of both thinking and writing, and that students can meet high school expectations when teachers slow down to show them how to write well. . . . what's most counter-cultural, and not really in the knowledge base, is how to develop students at the level of the sentence and all the ramifications that has in terms of thinking and content.[22]

It's vexing that hostility persists to a thoughtfully structured (not mindlessly regimented) curriculum, one that increases in complexity from the level of the word upward. One would be hard pressed to find a more avowed critic of cultural hegemony than the militant Italian Communist Antonio Gramsci—yet what did Gramsci say about education?

One has to inculcate certain habits of diligence, precision, poise (even physical poise), ability to concentrate on specific subjects, which cannot be acquired without the mechanical repetition of disciplined and methodical acts.[23]

(Gramsci also had nothing against learning Latin and Greek!) Erasmus insisted that pleasure can—indeed ought to—emerge from disciplined exercise: *If a gentle method of instruction is used, the process of education will resemble play more than work.*[24]

The humanist education put an

obvious emphasis upon both play of the mind and word-play. The grammar-school boy should never have been at a loss to play with any word or idea or—what was much the same—to develop any

[22] See Katrina Schwartz, "Is It Time to Go Back to Basics with Writing Instruction?" February 20, 2017, KQED: https://www.kqed.org/mindshift/47069/is-it-time-to-go -back-to-basics-with-writing-instruction. New Dorp follows the methods of Judith Hochman, who asserts, *It is insulting to the students to assume that the topic has to be about their own lives in order for the assignment to be interesting. Atlantic*, September 26, 2012.

[23] *Selections from the Prison Notebooks of Antonio Gramsci*, ed. and trans. Quintin Hoare and Geoffrey Nowell Smith (International Publishers, 1971), 37.

[24] *De pueris instituendis* [On Education for Children], in *Collected Works: Literary and Educational Writings 4*, ed. J. K. Sowards (University of Toronto Press, 1985), 324.

word or idea systematically. Tudor exuberance of language and expression was not accidental, but programmed.[25]

Such playful exuberance was achieved through the *Progymnasmata*'s fourteen steps of fable, narrative, saying, maxim, refutation, confirmation, commonplace, encomium, invective, comparison, characterization, description, thesis, and law. What an inspiring variety, in contrast to the *weary, stale, flat, and unprofitable* "five paragraph essay" into which the AP exam has contorted expository writing.[26]

Let's take one representative exercise:

11 CHARACTERIZATION *(êthopoeia)*: imitation of the character of someone

This makes you impersonate another persona in a hypothetical scenario. The goal is to *imitate that you may be different.*[27] Today, we tell students to "find their voice." Tudor educators did the opposite: sound like someone else—for instance, a grieving woman from the mythological past, *the words Niobe would say over her dead children*, which might lead a son to think of this:

A little month, or e'er those shoes were old
With which she followed my poor father's body,
Like Niobe all tears.

Or *the words Hecuba would say at the fall of Troy*, which might lead a student to think of this:

What's Hecuba to him or he to her
That he should weep for her?[28]

---

[25] Walter Ong, *Rhetoric, Romance, and Technology* (Cornell University Press, 2012), 63.

[26] *Hamlet* (1.2.133). See John Warner, *Why They Can't Write* (Johns Hopkins University Press, 2018). On the corrosive power of thinking in bullet points, see Edward Tufte's *The Cognitive Style of Powerpoint: Pitching Out Corrupts from Within* (Graphics Press, 2003): http://www.edwardtufte.com/tufte/powerpoint.

[27] Edward P. J. Corbett, "The Theory and Practice of Imitation in Classical Rhetoric," *College Composition and Communication* 22, no. 3 (October 1971): 250.

[28] *Hamlet* (1.2.147–49; 2.2.478–79).

In these cases, Hamlet ends up thinking about someone *pretending* to mourn.

Exercises in *êthopoeia* encouraged a rural English schoolboy to envisage what it might be like to occupy a different gender, in a different nation, observing a different religion, within a different era, under duress of different events. What we now call "empathy," or feeling with another, would have been more familiar to Shakespeare as "fellowship"—making others *copartners*, whether in pain or pleasure.[29] In the mid-seventeenth century, Margaret Cavendish lauded Shakespeare's ability to

> Express to the Life all Sorts of Persons, of what Quality, Profession, Degree, Breeding, or Birth soever; nor did he want Wit to Express the Divers, and Different Humours, or Natures, or Several Passions in Mankind; and so Well he hath Express'd in his Playes all Sorts of Persons, as one would think he had been Transformed into every one of those Persons he hath Described.[30]

A century later, Elizabeth Montagu concurred that Shakespeare *could throw his soul into the body of another man, and be at once possessed of his sentiments, adopt his passions, and rise to all the functions and feelings of his situation.*[31]

"Theory of mind" is our modern term for this kind of projection—as when Sir Thomas More rebukes the unruly London mob, urging them to imagine themselves in the position of *wretched strangers* (that is, refugees): *Whither would you go? . . . Why, you must needs be strangers . . . what would you think / To be thus used?*[32]

---

[29] *The Rape of Lucrece*, line 789. Paul Bloom and Fritz Breithaupt have raised cautions about appealing to "empathy" as a salve for social ills; Namwali Serpell addresses the issue (via Arendt) in "The Banality of Empathy," *New York Review of Books*, March 2, 2019: https://www.nybooks.com/daily/2019/03/02/the-banality-of-empathy/.

[30] Letter 123 of *CCXI Sociable Letters Written by the Thrice Noble, Illustrious, and Excellent Princess, the Lady Marchioness of Newcastle* (1664).

[31] *An Essay on the Writings and Genius of Shakespeare* (1769), 37.

[32] A facsimile of this speech, argued to be written in Shakespeare's hand, can be viewed online, along with recitations by Ian McKellan, Harriet Walter, and other actors and refugees: https://qz.com/786163/the-banned-400-year-old-shakespearean-speech-being-used-for-refugee-rights-today/; https://www.youtube.com/watch?v=4Bss2or4n74.

A letter from a former student renewed my appreciation of how this can be exercised through verse. Christopher Grubb, now a physician, related how a sonnet he had memorized inspires his approach to patients. In sonnet 73, the speaker compares his waning life to a tree, shedding its leaves:

That time of year thou mayst in me behold
When yellow leaves, or none, or few do hang
Upon those boughs which shake against the cold,
Bare ruined choirs where late the sweet birds sang.

Talk about useless knowledge! Or is it? Shakespeare enacts a double empathy here—that's to say, the speaker (me) imagines the addressee (thou) imagining the declining speaker: *That time of year thou mayst in me behold.* (He even tinkers with thought in action, moving from *some* leaves, then to *no* leaves, and back to *few* leaves, recoiling from the brink of his own mortality.) Meditating upon this poem strengthened Chris's capacity for projecting himself into the lives of others.[33] As Zadie Smith marvels:

> Shakespeare sees always both sides of a thing. . . . In his plays he is woman, man, black, white, believer, heretic, Catholic, Protestant, Jew, Muslim. . . . He understood what fierce, singular certainty creates, and what it destroys. In response, he made himself . . . speak truth plurally.[34]

As social media continues to isolate us into idiosyncratic, self-echoing units, we could all benefit from a bit more such fellowship today—more *speaking truth plurally.*

As we saw in the previous chapter, this era valued an imitation so pure that it resembled nothing other than the source itself, as in "double translation." On the other hand, the era valued imitation so extravagant that it threatened to dissolve into verbal profusion,

---

[33] William Empson reads these same lines at the opening of his ingenious *Seven Types of Ambiguity* (1930; New Directions, 1966), 3.

[34] "Speaking in Tongues," *New York Review of Books,* February 26, 2009.

as in Erasmus's *De copia*. *Copia* gives us "copy"—what (thanks to Xerox) we take for an exact reproduction.

Yet *copia* then was more akin to the copiousness that we associate with a horn of plenty, or "cornucopia." In Thomas Elyot's 1538 *Dictionary*, the word was synonymous with *plentie, eloquence, power, leaue, or licence, multitude*. Another word for *copia* ought to be "resourcefulness"—the ingenuity to make something out of the resources you have (and being full of resources in the first place).

In a fireworks display of verbal agility, Erasmus rings the changes on the phrase *tuae litterae me magnopere delectarunt, Your letter has pleased me greatly*, which he varies through different verbs, adjectives, word order . . . you name it. How many different ways can you say "the same thing"?

> Your letter mightily pleased me.
> To a wonderful degree did your letter please me.
> Me exceedingly did your letter please.
> By your letter was I mightily pleased.
> I was exceedingly pleased by your letter.
> Your epistle exhilarated me intensely.
> I was intensely exhilarated by your epistle.
> Your brief note refreshed my spirits in no small measure.
> I was in no small measure refreshed in spirit by your grace's hand.
> From your affectionate letter I received unbelievable pleasure.
> Your affectionate letter brought me unbelievable pleasure.
> Your pages engendered in me an unfamiliar delight.
> I conceived a wonderful delight from your pages.
> Your lines conveyed to me the greatest joy.
> The greatest joy was brought to me by your lines.
> We derived great delight from your excellency's letter.[35]

. . . and over 130 more variations![36] As if that wasn't enough, these scores of changes were followed by another 200 variations on

---

[35] *Copia: Foundations of the Abundant Style*, in *Literary and Educational Writings 1 and 2*, trans. Betty I. Knott (University of Toronto Press, 1978), 427ff.

[36] A former student, Adrian Scaife, recounted how a friend was tasked with developing one hundred-plus versions of a slogan for an ad agency, *even if you think you've already come*

semper dum vivam tui meminero (*I will always love*—oops, *remember*—*you*).

Erasmus understood that *affectation of Copia is dangerous* (the title of his first chapter), and knew that you needed to study *both* words (*verba*) and matter (*res*). Shakespeare loved this kind of play, even as he mocked its pretentious excesses: *caelo, the sky, the welkin, the heaven . . . terra, the soil, the land, the earth.*[37]

My students laugh when they see the over-the-top list of permutations on *Your letter has pleased me greatly*. But *copia's* exercises in variation make you appreciate (and expand) the range of possibility, in order to say it *right*. Per Orwell, if you just let *the ready-made phrases come crowding in* to your mind,

> they will construct your sentences for you—even think your thoughts for you, to a certain extent—and at need they will perform the important service of partially concealing your meaning even from yourself. It is at this point that the special connection between politics and the debasement of language becomes clear.[38]

Confucius gets at the heart of verbal precision that *copia* exercises force you to refine:

> If language is not correct, then what is said is not what is meant; if what is said is not what is meant, then what must be done remains undone; if this remains undone, morals and art will deteriorate; if justice goes astray, the people will stand about in helpless confusion. Hence there must be no arbitrariness in what is said. This matters above everything.[39]

Words matter.

---

up with the winner. In *99 Variations on a Proof* (Princeton University Press, 2019), Philip Ording tackles the same theorem through a witty array of approaches, just as Raymond Queneau's *Exercises in Style* (1947) retold the same banal anecdote (about riding a bus) in kaleidoscopic variety.

[37] *Love's Labor's Lost* (4.2.5–6).

[38] "Politics and the English Language" (1946), in *The Orwell Reader: Fiction, Essays, and Reportage* (Mariner Books, 1961), 362.

[39] *Analects* (13.3), as paraphrased by Erich Heller, in "Satirist in the Modern World," *Times Literary Supplement*, May 8, 1953.

Tibetan Buddhist nuns practicing their debating skills, Dolma Ling Nunnery and Institute, India, 2013. Image courtesy of Olivier Adam.

10

OF CONVERSATION

Conversation is the laboratory and workshop of the student.
—Ralph Waldo Emerson, *The Natural Method of Mental Philosophy* (1858)

Kenneth Burke, one of my heroes, dropped out of college to school himself in 1920s Greenwich Village. Over the next seventy years, his roving wit contributed to fields as disparate as sociology, religion, historiography, composition, and even Shakespeare studies. A rhetorician at heart, he had a wordsmith's knack for an arresting metaphor—as in this one, about how thought unfolds:

> Imagine that you enter a parlor. You come late. When you arrive, others have long preceded you, and they are engaged in a heated discussion, a discussion too heated for them to pause and tell you exactly what it is about. In fact, the discussion had already begun long before any of them got there, so that no one present is qualified to retrace for you all the steps that had gone before. You listen for a while, until you decide that you have caught the tenor of the argument; then you put in your oar. Someone answers; you answer him; another comes to your defense; another aligns himself against you, to either the embarrassment or gratification of your opponent, depending upon the quality of your ally's assistance. However, the discussion is interminable. The hour grows late, you must depart. And you do depart, with the discussion still vigorously in progress.[1]

---

[1] *The Philosophy of Literary Form* (Louisiana State University Press, 1941), 110–11. The best introduction to Burke's quicksilver mind remains "Literature as Equipment for Living,"

Burke dramatizes the *unending conversation* of intellectual history—how we enter a conceptual debate, stake a claim, and (eventually) depart. Insofar as it starts in the middle of things and has no conclusive ending, it sounds a lot like a Socratic dialogue! Burke's *parlor* scenario leans upon the sociable arts of *conversation*, including both disputation and persuasion, but with more benign, irenic overtones. It covers language not only in the court, the school, the government, or the market, but also in the personal and aesthetic realms.

Shakespeare's era prized conversation's capacity *to rub and polish our brains by contact with those of others*.[2] Elaborating on medieval and classical genres, dialogue prevailed in philosophical discourse, political treatises, protoscientific tracts, scholarly apparatuses (with marginal glosses and footnotes in dialogue with the main text), practical manuals for anything from "how to learn a language" to "how to die." Even reading a book on your own was figured as a *conversation with the deceased*, where you *listen to the dead* with your eyes.[3]

Religious instruction was often staged in the form of a catechism: *Make questions and by them answer*.[4] Think of Falstaff's skeptical turn on "honor," rephrased here in a Q&A:

Q. Can honor set to a leg?
A. No.
Q. Or an arm?
A. No.
Q. Or take away the grief of a wound?
A. No.

---

gathered in this same volume (293–304). I've edited *Kenneth Burke on Shakespeare* (Parlor Press, 2007).

[2] Michel de Montaigne, "Of the Education of Children," in *Essays and Selected Writings: A Bilingual Edition*, trans. Donald M. Frame (Columbia University Press, 1963), 41.

[3] Francisco de Quevedo, Poem 131, translated by George Mariscal, in *Contradictory Subjects* (Cornell University Press, 1991), 69.

[4] *Othello* (3.4.14–15).

Q. Honor hath no skill in surgery then?

A. No.

Q. What is honor?

A. A word.

Q. What is in that word "honor"? What is that "honor"?

A. Air. A trim reckoning!

Q. Who hath it?

A. He that died o'Wednesday.

Q. Doth he feel it?

A. No.

Q. Doth he hear it?

A. No.

Q. 'Tis insensible, then?

A. Yea, to the dead.

Q. But will it not live with the living?

A. No.

Q. Why?

A. Detraction will not suffer it. Therefore I'll none of it. Honor is a mere scutcheon. And so ends my catechism.[5]

Our *internal* dialogue—our *conscience* ("thinking with")—is rhetorical too, according to Isocrates:

> The same arguments which we use in persuading others when we speak in public, we employ also when we deliberate in our own thoughts; and while we call eloquent those who are able to speak before a crowd, we regard as sage those who most skilfully debate their problems in their own minds.[6]

A good motto for this period would be Erasmus's audacious modification of the opening words of the Gospel of John: *In principio erat sermo*. This is familiar to us in English as *In the beginning was*

---

[5] *1 Henry IV* (5.1.130–39).

[6] *Nicocles or the Cyprians* (5–8), cited in Celeste Michelle Condit and John Louis Lucaites, *Crafting Equality* (University of Chicago Press, 1993), xi.

the word (travestied by Samuel Beckett: *In the beginning was the pun*).[7] Since Jerome in the fourth century, this phrase had been Latinized as *In principio erat verbum*—*verbum* as equivalent to the Greek *logos*, or "word." Yet *logos* could also mean "discourse" or "reasoning" (hence "logic"). Erasmus, seeking like Burke to socialize and generalize that *logos*, instead offered *In principio erat sermo*—which gives us our word "sermon," but means something more akin to informal "conversation."

In the beginning was the <u>conversation</u>. Given this beginning, it's not surprising that Erasmus held that *the skill of flawless speech is best acquired both from the conversation and company of correct speakers and also from incessant reading of eloquent authors.* In other words: dialogue with both present and past.[8] If *through others we become ourselves,*[9] how might we envision a pedagogy that placed a premium on conversation?

It would be suffused with *questions*. And not so-called rhetorical questions in the pejorative sense (we all know what *those* look like, right?). Rather, *generative* questions, *beautiful* questions, to catalyze further thought. When Hamlet launches into *To be or not to be: that is the <u>question</u>,* he's alluding to the pedagogical practice of setting up "To X or not to X" disputes, then arguing on both sides (*in utramque partem*) of the question: *on the one hand, this; on the other hand, that.* (Even *to be or not to bée* was one of the "questions" in logic textbooks from the 1570s onward.)[10]

Many of Shakespeare's soliloquies are generated by this kind of either/or premise, weighing two courses of action, as are many of Francis Bacon's essays (*To marry or not to marry* was another con-

---

[7] *Murphy* (Grove Press, 1952), 65.

[8] *De rationi studii,* cited in *Principles of Letter-Writing: A Bilingual Text of Justi Lipsii Epistolica,* trans. R. V. Young and M. Thomas Hester (Southern Illinois University Press, 1996), 61.

[9] L. S. Vygotsky, *The Collected Works of L. S. Vygotsky,* vol. 4 (1931, Plenum Press, 1997), 105.

[10] *Hamlet* (3.1.55). Cited in Peter Stallybrass, "Against Thinking," *PMLA* 122, no. 5 (October 2007): 1580–87.

ventional question). The goal of this bi-vocal argumentation was not an equivocating denial of the truth, but a probing, conversational clarification of the truth: *The sole object of our discussions is by arguing on both sides to draw out and give shape to some result that may be either true or the nearest possible approximation to the truth.*[11]

Expansion, unlike narrowness of mind, demands agility. You must *occupy* (at least) two sides of the question (or dilemma, or paradox) with equal vigor and rigor, inducing a nimble, antidoctrinal equipoise. Erasmus even advised that students compose "recantations" of arguments they had just completed!—a kind of self-debate. Such a system cultivates the kind of ethical, antidogmatic broadmindedness advocated by John Stuart Mill:

> He who knows only his own side of the case, knows little of that. His reasons may be good, and no one may have been able to refute them. But if he is equally unable to refute the reasons on the opposite side; if he does not so much as know what they are, he has no ground for preferring either opinion.[12]

Everyone from Greek sophists to the Buddhist nuns illustrating this chapter has always known that one of the best pedagogical tricks is to make students strenuously argue a position—and then force them to argue the opposite. To cultivate conversation at its highest level, you are asked to "stand" in the position of your opponent.

At Xerox's research center, one of the most innovative places in the world in the 1970s (if you've ever used a computer mouse, thank them), this kind of structured debate was routine:

> Formal discussions [were] designed to train their people on how to fight properly over ideas and not egos. . . . Before each meeting,

[11] Cicero, *De natura deourum & academica*, trans. H. Rackham (Harvard University Press, 1933), 475.
[12] *On Liberty* (Longmans, Green, and Co., 1867), 21.

one person, known as "the dealer," was selected as the speaker. The speaker would present his idea and then try to defend it against a room of engineers and scientists determined to prove him wrong. Such debates helped improve products under development and sometimes resulted in wholly new ideas for future pursuit.[13]

Civil, productive argument helps you articulate where you stand, and where to go from here. You can see an embodied version of this *stand*ing in *1 Henry IV*, when Prince Harry directs a mini-play in which Falstaff will *stand for my father and examine me upon the particulars of my life.* After a bit of mutual ribbing, they swap places; Harry then commands, *Do thou stand for me, and I'll play my father.* Falstaff accedes: *And here I stand. Judge, my masters.*[14]

As Launce jokes in *The Two Gentlemen of Verona*: *Why, "stand-under" and "under-stand" is all one* (2.5.28). That is, understanding comes from holding your ground in conversation with others, *to look upon the same world from one another's standpoint, to see the same in very different and frequently opposing aspects.* In Frederick Douglass's words, "To *understand* . . . a man must *stand under.*"[15]

Position taking, position making, position forsaking. In a similar spirit, the Long Now Foundation sponsors debates that mandate this kind under-*standing*; before you are permitted to present your position, you must first *present the best form of the other person's argument.*[16] This kind of thinking demands that we suspend our own ego, and be *capable of being in uncertainties, Mysteries, doubts.*[17]

[13] David Burkus's account in *The Myths of Creativity* (Jossey-Bass, 2013), 154.

[14] *1 Henry IV* (2.4.342–43, 393–94, 399).

[15] Hannah Arendt, *Between Past and Future* (Penguin, 2006), 51. *Autobiographies*, edited by Henry Louis Gates, Jr. (Library of America, 1994), 310.

[16] The phrase is from Chana Messinger, cited in Alan Jacobs's companionable *How to Think* (Currency, 2017), 108.

[17] John Keats, to George and Tom Keats, December 21, 1817, in *The Letters of John Keats, 1814–1821*, ed. Hyder Edward Rollins (Harvard University Press, 1958), 1:136.

Once you are familiar with Shakespeare's training in thinking through many sides of any question, you can see how conducive such a mind-set would be to the verbal give-and-take that constitutes the heart of drama. Characters themselves embody questioning, posed in tension with one another—as if we were watching a *mind in motion.*[18]

Thinking through questions *tempers* your thought—that is, both *strengthens* and *moderates* it. Hard interrogation is ever more urgent in an age awash in data. As Picasso said about computers, *they are useless. They can only give you answers.*[19]

We develop better questions through conversation with the past, and through good teaching, which is *more a giving of right questions than a giving of right answers.*[20] An educational program that models, celebrates, and habituates multisided interrogation is the kind of education needed now, more than ever, as device-tethered students are *having a hard time with the give-and-take of face-to-face conversation.*[21] Their decline in conversation starts early, as devices put a screen between them and other people. Third grade teacher Launa Hall regrets her classroom's introduction of iPads:

> These young humans are not great conversationalists.... They need time to learn communication skills—how to hold your own and how to get along with others. They need to talk and listen and talk some more at school, both with peers and with adults who can model conversation skills.... jumping from the "sage on the stage" teaching model to a screen for each kid skips over critical territory in between, where children learn from, and build their social skills with, one another.... Teachers striving to preserve

[18] James Longenbach, "The Sound of Shakespeare Thinking," in *The Oxford Handbook of Shakespeare's Poetry*, ed. Jonathan Post (Oxford University Press, 2013), 76.

[19] William Fifield, "Pablo Picasso: A Composite Interview," *Paris Review* 32 (Summer-Fall 1964): 62.

[20] Joseph Albers, *Interaction of Color* (1963; Yale University Press, 2006), 70.

[21] Sherry Turkle, *Reclaiming Conversation* (Penguin, 2015), 171.

precious space for conversation are not lazy, or afraid of change, or obstructionist.[22]

The Tudor classroom embedded further reciprocity through theater, including reading Latin plays by Terence, Plautus, and Seneca; performing holiday dramas of the students' composition; and delivering declamations. I love Richard Mulcaster's advocacy of *Loudspeaking*, designed to stretch tonal range by oscillating between *harsh and hard, now smooth and sweet*[23]—audio plyometrics! so that when the time came, you could speak without notes, and with confidence.

Not that everyone appreciated the many virtues of this practice in performance. Ben Jonson's *Staple of News* (1626) has a character named "Gossip Censure" (Jonson was merciless in naming) whinge: *They make all their scholars play-boys! . . . Do we pay our money for this? We send them to learn their grammar, and their Terence, and they learn their play-books.*

This could have been brayed yesterday by a legislator mocking "worthless" degrees. But Censure misses the point on several levels—the first being that Terence, taken to stand in for generic Latin learning, *is a playwright*. Again, as with *êthopoeia*, the goal was sympathetic projection into other subject positions, *as if they themselves were the persons which did speak in that dialogue, and so in every other speech, to imagine themselves to have occasion to utter the very same things.*[24]

This projection was refined in letter-writing schemes promoted by Erasmus, Lipsius, and others. Students had to put themselves in conversations that they hadn't yet encountered: a letter of condolence, a letter requesting patronage, a letter to a distant friend, a

[22] "I Gave My Students iPads—Then Wished I Could Take Them Back," *Washington Post*, December 2, 2015.

[23] John Brinsley, *Positions* (1581), cited by Bertram Leon Joseph, in *Acting Shakespeare* (1960; Routledge, 2014), 10.

[24] Brinsley, *Ludus Literarius or, The Grammar School* (1612), cited in Lois Potter, *The Life of William Shakespeare* (Wiley-Blackwell, 2012), 34.

letter to a dead writer or even a fictive entity. Indeed, many of these epistolary lessons still hold for email today:

1. Keep it brief, make it simple; 2. Write as you speak; 3. Don't be afraid to grovel; 4. Be spontaneous, be free; 5. Tell it like it is; 6. Write back swiftly, but carefully; 7. Emotional blackmail may work with your parents; 8. Be more polite than you really want to be; 9. Don't forget the paper clip; 10. The young get all the blame; PS If all else fails, send fish.[25]

While this was formal training for bureaucratic careers, the letter-writing exercises far exceeded their "utility" beyond mere training. Projecting yourself into futures that you haven't experienced—and might never—both required and enabled mental discipline. For this to happen, there has to be an extensive and sophisticated vocabulary. Their education forced them to develop, not shrink, the vocabulary available to them (think back to *copia*—it's telling that the phrase Erasmus riffs on is the utterly formulaic *Your letter has pleased me greatly*). This enabled them to notice and communicate shades of meaning, adjusted to the occasion and audience. It's hard to overestimate how useful, indeed *essential* all this is: the future's unknown, but individuals and societies are bound to face complex issues. An education in the Shakespearean language arts has a Boy Scout quality: *Be Prepared*. Its advantage lies in the fact that it works, stretches, and enlarges the tool most characteristic of the human: the *mind*.

[25] Simon Garfield, "10 Old Letter-Writing Tips that Work for Emails" (October 28, 2013): http://www.bbc.co.uk/news/magazine-24609533.

Katsushika Hokusai, detail of handscroll with miscellaneous images (1839). Freer Gallery of Art and Arthur M. Sackler Gallery, Smithsonian Institution, Washington, DC: Gift of Charles Lang Freer, F1902.42.

11

OF STOCK

I have stolen ideas from every book I have ever read.
My principle in researching for a novel is "Read like a
butterfly, write like a bee," and if this story contains any honey,
it is entirely because of the quality of the nectar
I found in the work of better writers.
—Philip Pullman, acknowledgments to *The Amber Spyglass* (2001)

Nobel laureate Joseph Brodsky once taught a poem by Osip Mandelstam, Brodsky's hero who died in Stalin's gulag. Mandelstam alluded to Ovid. When Brodsky asked how many of his American students knew Ovid, no one answered. His stunned response: *You've been cheated.*[1]

Brodsky didn't scold his students for the gaps in their reading. Being human and finite, no one can read everything. Instead, Brodsky shifted the blame: someone had cheated *them* of their cultural inheritance—and it was his own generation.

Teachers select things students ought to know before progressing to advanced study. That's the nature of teaching. But many of us have become allergic to the very idea of anything akin to a common stock of knowledge, claiming that requiring *any* particular reading would be "privileging."

Yes, it would be—just as it's privileging for a chemist to expect her students to learn the periodic table, or for a law school professor to expect future lawyers to know the Constitution. At the

---

[1] Peter Scotto, "Comics and the Bard; Students, Cheated," *New York Times*, April 1, 1998.

outset of medical school, future astronaut Mae C. Jemison resented the endless array of facts she was expected to memorize. But she overcame her aversion once she recognized that *you actually want your doctor to know this stuff cold! You don't want them going into the ER and then looking stuff up while you're there bleeding!*[2]

To cite Brodsky again: *There are worse crimes than burning books—one is not reading them.*[3]

You've been cheated—that's the same phrase Earl Shorris deployed when describing how he designed a program for disadvantaged students: *You've been cheated. Rich people learn the humanities; you didn't. . . . the humanities are one of the ways to become political.*[4]

Brodsky was teaching privileged (wealthy) students, who had not had Ovid privileged (selected) for them. For someone who had grown up under the educational deprivations of an oppressive regime, this was unfathomable. That doesn't mean any heritage is ever static, or invariable. Every tradition is animated by ongoing debate, and there's never a uniform consensus about what it includes from era to era, from people to people.

But it's real, it endures, and it surpasses the individual, as a character in Willa Cather's *Death Comes to the Archbishop* observes: *A soup like this is not the work of one man. It is the result of a constantly refined tradition. There are nearly a thousand years of history in this soup.*[5]

Modernity, for better and for worse, entails the violent razing of tradition, as all that is solid melts into air. Or in Henry Ford's hard-nosed Americanese: *We don't want tradition. We want to live in the present and the only history that is worth a tinker's dam is the history we make today.*[6]

---

[2] Commonwealth Club of California (December 13, 2016).

[3] "New Poet Laureate Meets the Press," *Library of Congress Information Bulletin*, June 17, 1991, 225.

[4] *The Art of Freedom* (Norton, 2013), 23.

[5] *Death Comes for the Archbishop* (1927; Knopf, 1962), 39.

[6] Interview with Charles N. Wheeler, *Chicago Tribune*, May 25, 1916.

To a degree, this is freeing: we've become artists of our own lives, with no precedent to constrain us. Yet the collapse of tradition also leaves us unmoored in a contextless world where individualism finds its expression via the *freedom to choose what is always the same.*[7]

A sense of "common stock" was long considered a communal property: something *from* which you have a right to *draw*. Stock was also something *to* which you could *contribute*:

- *As an individual every one of us contributes his goods, his person, his life, to the common stock.*

—Jean Jacques Rousseau, *Emile* (1762)

- *I think every one ought to contribute to the common Stock, and to have no other Scruple or Shyness, about the receiving of Truth.*

—John Locke to William Molyneux (1692)

- *they may see what they have, what they may question, and what they may add and contribute to the common stock.*

—Francis Bacon, *The Great Instauration* (1620)

- *we have also contributed something from our own stores to the common stock.*

— Cicero, *De inventione* (c. 84 BCE)[8]

"Stock" evolves from the material sense of "stores" or "stuff" (as in "livestock" or even "wordstock") to the more metaphorical sense of a stock of concepts, or knowledge, held in common. Brodsky, or Mandelstam, or Shakespeare, or you can trade upon this mutable yet real stock of knowledge, reconfiguring Ovid (and others)

---

[7] Theodor W. Adorno and Max Horkheimer, *Dialectic of Enlightenment* (1947), trans. John Cumming (Verso, 1997), 167.

[8] *Emile, or Education* (J. M. Dent & Sons, 1966), 424; *Some familiar Letters between Mr Locke and several of his friends* (1737), 11; preface to "The Great Renewal," *Francis Bacon: The New Organon*, ed. Lisa Jardine and Michael Silverthorne (Cambridge University Press, 2000), 11; *The Fourteen Orations against Marcus Antonius*, trans. C. D. Yonge (George Bell & Sons, 1890), 310.

through quotations, echoes, and revisions, adding "new stock . . . to humanity."[9] Shakespeare's peers even called upon this Ovidian stock in praising him: *The sweet witty soul of Ovid lives in mellifluous & honey-tongued Shakespeare.*[10]

My point isn't that you should read Ovid. (Though you're only cheating yourself if you don't—it's great stuff!) My point is that we've given up on any common stock.

Some scholars scorn what they caricature as a *banking concept* of education, in which an oppressive teacher deposits knowledge in a passive, ignorant student, *alienated like the slave.*[11] There's much that's confused here. For one, deposit-only "banking" isn't even how *actual* banking works, which requires the flow of capital stock. And is education ever so unidirectional? Overcorrecting this false scenario throws out the stock with the bathwater. Real education oscillates between knowledge acquisition and knowledge application, between stock and exercise.

The secret of stock is that it gives you the base to make something else. This is true whether it's Cather's soup stock or the wonderful stew of culture more generally. *Knowledge matters.* It provides the scaffolding for future inquiry. In the most extreme example, if you knew no words in a language, having a dictionary wouldn't help you in the least, since every definition would lead you to more words you didn't know. The best predictor for success in reading comprehension is . . . vocabulary.[12]

Without a stock of knowledge, it's difficult to process (much less gather and build) more knowledge. It's called the "Matthew Effect": the perverse way in which those who have, shall receive even more in abundance; those who have less, shall receive less.

[9] Ralph Waldo Emerson, *Success*, in *The Works of Ralph Waldo Emerson*, vol. 7, *Society and Solitude* (Fireside edition, 1909), 7:308.

[10] Francis Meres, *Palladis Tamia, Wits Treasury* (1598).

[11] Paolo Freire, *Pedagogy of the Oppressed* (1973; Continuum, 1993), 53.

[12] See Timothy Rasinski, Nancy Padak, and Joanna Newton, "The Roots of Comprehension": http://www.ascd.org/publications/educational-leadership/feb17/vol74/num05/The-Roots-of-Comprehension.aspx.

Without a structured and graduated curriculum, the gap in vocabulary between poor students and wealthy students not only
persists, but widens. The principled yet wrongheaded antipathy to
intellectual stock reinforces socioeconomic inequality; *we neglect
stock at our peril.*[13]

Tradition derives from the Latin *traditio*—that which is *handed*
down to you for safekeeping. Part of our innate skepticism of tradition derives from admirable impulses: we don't want someone else
telling us what to do; we want to decide for ourselves. We reject a
thoughtless adherence to tradition, just as we reject (I hope,
though of late I'm not so certain) the thoughtlessness that accom-
panies authoritarianism. Yet educational *authority* (including the
stock of tradition) is not the same thing as political *authoritarianism*. We all lose when we conflate these categories.

Erasmus knew you had to cultivate widely read teachers, so they
could in turn select the best stock for their students:

> As regards the choice of *material*, it is essential that from the out-
> set the child be made acquainted only with the best that is avail-
> able. This implies that the Master is competent to recognise the
> best in the mass of erudition open to him, which in turn signifies
> that he has read far more widely than the range of authors to be
> taught by him. This applies even to the tutor of beginners. . . . it is
> only a Master of ability, insight, and wide culture, to whom such a
> method is possible. A store of pertinent quotations is the product
> of careful reading.[14]

Or as Gandhi once put it, *I want the cultures of all lands to be blown
about my house as freely as possible.*[15]

---

[13] Robin Sloan speaks here of our world's imbalance balance between "stock" (static
value) and "flow" (rate of change): http://snarkmarket.com/2010/4890. His point is even
more harrowing for those structurally excluded from "stock."

[14] *Desiderius Erasmus, Concerning the Aim and Method of Education*, trans. William
Harrison Woodward (Cambridge University Press, 1904), 166, 174.

[15] *All Men Are Brothers: Autobiographical Reflections*, ed. Krishna Kripalani (1921;
Navajivan, 1995), 142.

Because widely read teachers know how to connect the past to the future, they can help the student figure out what to do now:

> The more you dwell in the past and future, the thicker your band-width, the more solid your persona. But the narrower your sense of Now, the more tenuous you are.[16]

Wide reading helps teachers cultivate judgment, so that they can select from *the best in the mass of erudition*.[17] While we must always argue about what counts as "the best," we now seem to confuse informed *judgment* with being capriciously *judgmental*, a loaded word—just as we confuse a practical *regimen* with an oppressive *regime*, or *conserving* with a bogeyman of being *conservative*. (If anything, I'd characterize this kind of education as *conversative*, as in: committed to conversation.)

Even though they do not agree on *which* models to imitate, thinkers from Quintilian to John of Salisbury to Milton concurred that there *were* models worth imitating, *just like a carpenter who works as an apprentice and studies the master*.[18] Their educational programs were founded on an aspiration to do better. Thoreau conveys the urgency of this aspiration: *Read the best books first, or you may not have a chance to read them at all*.[19]

Schools today increasingly assign contemporary nonfiction ex-cerpts, in the vague hope that exposing students to such "informa-tional text" will make them better readers. (Spoiler: it doesn't.) Even journalists don't recommend their own writing for this pur-pose! When *Time* columnist Joel Stein received emails from stu-dents who had been assigned his articles, he implored them to

[16] Thomas Pynchon, *Gravity's Rainbow* (1973), cited by Alan Jacobs, "To Survive Our High-Speed Society, Cultivate 'Temporal Bandwidth,'" *Guardian*, June 16, 2018.

[17] Erasmus again: 166.

[18] William Faulkner, classroom statements at the University of Mississippi, 1947, cited in James B. Meriwether and Michael Millgate, *Lion in the Garden* (Random House, 1968), 55.

[19] *The Writings of Henry David Thoreau 1. A Week on the Concord and Merrimack Rivers* (1849; Houghton Mifflin and Company, 1906), 98.

transfer high schools immediately! To one that teaches Shakespeare and Homer instead of the insightful commentary of a first-rate, unconventionally handsome modern wit![20]

Simon Barnes offers a similar response to inquiries from aspiring sports journalists: *You could either spend three years reading Shakespeare and Joyce, or three years reading me. Work it out for yourself.*[21]

Take stock: the contemporary analogue might a blog, a Tumblr, an advertising agency's "swipe file," Beyoncé's "memory bank."[22] Stock grants us *inventio*, a word that gave us not only "invention" but also "inventory." Cartoon images of inventors depict a light-bulb flashing above the head of a solitary genius. But, as Keith Richards admits in his autobiography, *nothing came from itself.* He was endorsing Mary Wollstonecraft Shelley's preface to her second edition of *Frankenstein*: *Invention, it must be humbly admitted, does not consist in creating out of void.*

Or maybe it was Jean-Auguste-Dominique Ingres's injunction that painters must build on the creativity of predecessors: *You don't get anything from nothing.* To be fair, I should acknowledge the earlier Sir Joshua Reynolds, who pointed out that *invention, strictly speaking, is little more than a new combination of those images which have been previously gathered and deposited in the memory; nothing can come of nothing.*[23]

Well, technically, Reynolds is quoting *King Lear*: *Nothing can be made out of nothing* (1.4.121). Wait, that's Lear, citing his own earlier rage: *Nothing will come of nothing* (1.1.88).

[20] "How I Replaced Shakespeare," *Time*, December 10, 2012: http://content.time.com /time/subscriber/article/0,33009,2130408-1,00.html.

[21] "Education Is Supposed to Make You Rich, Not Wealthy," *Times* (London), July 16, 2007.

[22] Jon Youshaei, "What Beyoncé & Shakespeare Have in Common" (2016): http:// www.everyvowel.com/beyonce-shakespeare-key-to-creativity-success-lemonade.

[23] Richards, *Life* (Little, Brown, 2010), 66; Shelley, *Frankenstein, or the Modern Prometheus* (1831; Wordsworth Editions, 1993), 3; Boyer d'Agen, ed., *Ingres, d'après une correspondance inédite* (Daragon, 1909), 91; Reynolds, *Discourses on the Fine Arts Delivered to the Students of the Royal Academy* (1769; William and Robert Chambers, 1853), 7.

Which alludes to the maxim *ex nihilo nihil fit*, found in sixteenth-century commonplace books. Which in turn lifts from Lucretius's *On the Nature of Things*. Who got it from Aristotle's *Physics*. Who derived it from Plato's *Sophist*. Who was familiar with Parmenides's *On Nature* . . . you get the point! We're all standing on the shoulders of giants.[24]

When rhetoricians spoke of *inventio*, they meant the first step in constructing an argument: making an *inventory* of your mind's stock of knowledge—your treasury of thoughts, your database of reading, which you can accumulate only through slow, deliberate study. You cannot transform tradition (a creative ideal) without first knowing it (a conserving ideal). Making an inventory must precede making an invention. Shakespeare's education furnished him with a stock of words, concepts, names, and plots that he would reinvent throughout his career. He had a *gift of telling a story (provided some one else told it to him first)*.[25]

Immersion in distant, difficult works enlarges your mind and your world, providing for a lifetime of expanded inquiry. A well-stocked mind is what prepares you for flashes of insight: *It is necessary to have all the materials of an invention in your head*; *The best geologist is he who has seen the most rocks*.[26]

But how does this all come together? How do *all these things work around in [your] head and somehow . . . jell?*[27]

Many have tried to describe how to move from the gathering of fragments into an assembled, new whole—that imperceptible transition from a latent state to an aha moment, when you *refash-*

---

[24] Even Isaac Newton's phrase "on the shoulders of giants" stands on the shoulders of previous quotations, a quixotic history wittily traced by Robert Merton, *On the Shoulders of Giants: The Post-Italianate Edition* (University of Chicago Press, 1993).

[25] George Bernard Shaw, "Blaming the Bard" (September 1896), in *Dramatic Opinions and Essays with an Apology*, ed. James Huneker, vol. 2 (Brentano's, 1922), 51–59.

[26] Gordon Gould, inventor of the laser, cited in Steven J. Paley, *The Art of Invention* (Prometheus Books, 2010), 55; Herbert Harold Read, *The Granite Controversy* (Murby, 1957), 430.

[27] George R. R. Martin, discussing how he lifts plots from Shakespeare; interviewed by Mikal Gilmore, *Rolling Stone*, April 23, 2014.

ion . . . materials already at hand, so that the relics of other[s] . . . are incorporated.[28] Graham Wallas, cofounder of the London School of Economics, described the stages of the creative process by turning to Duke Theseus's famous speech on the imagination:

> "Forms of things unknown" and "airy nothings" are vivid descriptions of the first appearance of Intimation; and "local habitation and a name" indicates the increasing verbal clearness of thought . . . Shakespeare was a much more conscious artist than many of his admirers believe.[29]

More simply: *You put two things together that have not been put together before. And the world is changed.*[30]

You might think of this combining as alchemical compounding; the artisanal craft of joinery (the carpenter's fitting of pieces); or even patchwork, stitching together scraps of used materials.[31] The most prevalent register for creative combination in Shakespeare's world was *horticultural*, the boundary of the natural and the artificial, shaped by human hands. Rhetorical manuals were titled *Gardens of Eloquence*; poetry anthologies were "gatherings" of "flowers" of verse. John Florio's translation of Montaigne addresses the reader by confessing that the best *but glean after others' harvest*.[32] Early feminist advocate Bathsua Makin went so far as to assert that *as plants in gardens excel those that grow wild . . . so [we] by liberal education are much better'd*.[33]

"Grafting" underscored the generative intermingling of branch

[28] Walter Pater's description of Shakespeare's creative process, in *The Works of Walter Pater*, vol. 5, *Appreciations, with an Essay on Style* (Macmillan, 1902), 182.

[29] *A Midsummer Night's Dream* (5.1.1–22). *The Art of Thought* (1926; Solis Press, 2014), 52.

[30] Julian Barnes, *Levels of Life* (Vintage, 2014), 3.

[31] See Tiffany Stern, "Introduction: Playwrights as Play-Patchers," in *Documents of Performance in Early Modern England* (Cambridge University Press, 2009), 1–7.

[32] "To the Courteous Reader" (1603), in *Shakespeare's Montaigne*, ed. Stephen Greenblatt and Peter G. Platt (New York Review Books, 2014), 6.

[33] *An Essay to Revive the Antient Education of Gentlewomen* (1673), in *Bathsua Makin, Woman of Learning*, ed. Frances Teague (Bucknell University Press, 1998), 113.

and tree, *and graffe them into a new stock*.[34] "Stock" was the exist-
ing archive of past texts or even practices, which is no threat to
the present, but rather a fertile *ground, / Set with rich grafts and
plants*.[35] According to Queen Elizabeth I, when we read, we

> pluck up the goodly green herbs of sentences by pruning; eat
> them by reading; chew them by musing; and lay them up at length
> in the high seat of memory by gathering them together.[36]

The pleasure of pruning, ingesting, digesting, and gathering con-
trasts with the disgust conveyed when students today say that
school forces them to "regurgitate" what they've taken in; this is
bulimic reading, at best. As one teacher laments, *We feed the knowledge to them, they puke it back up, and if it looks enough like what
went down, they get a grade*.[37] Montaigne likewise described an
incomplete education as vomiting, for we *disgorge what we eat in
the same condition it was swallowed*.[38]

Instead, the process of productive digestion ought to resemble
gathering nectar from many flowers and then transforming it into
honey, *as bees summarise the garden*:[39]

> The bees steal from this flower and that, but afterward turn their
> pilferings into honey, which is their own.... So the pupil will
> transform and fuse together the passages that he borrows from
> others, to make of them something entirely his own.[40]

[34] John Maplet, *A Greene Forest* (1567), 28.

[35] William Basse, *A Helpe to memory and discourse* (1620).

[36] Bodleian Ms. E Museo 242, cited in *Elizabeth I: Translations, 1544–1589*, edited by
Janel Mueller and Joshua Scodel (Chicago, 2009), 404. Aptly, Elizabeth plucked this quotation from a treatise attributed to Augustine—commonplacing at work again!

[37] David Finkle, "Models for Education: Education as Synthesis" (unpublished essay,
May 2017).

[38] *On the Education of Children*, trans. Charles Cotton (Doubleday, 1947), 145.

[39] Les Murray, "Nursing Home," in *Taller When Prone* (Black, 2010), 24. For an apian
anthology, see https://didostears.wordpress.com/351-2/.

[40] Montaigne, *Essays*, trans. J. M. Cohen (Harmondsworth, 1958), 56.

You are what you read. Or, as Helen Keller replied, when accused of plagiarism, *It is certain that I cannot always distinguish my own thoughts from those I read, because what I read becomes the very substance and text of my mind.*[41]

The honey metaphor corrects our naive notion that creation consists of making something from nothing. You need stock. John Coltrane concurred: *You've got to look back at the old things and see them in a new light.*[42] Just listen to him fuse experimental jazz, South Asian melodic modes, Russian music theory, and the ballad "Greensleeves" (already riffed on by Shakespeare!)[43] and you'll hear how engaging with the past *generates* rather than *limits*. Improvisation contributes to the common stock.

Why develop *so wide a variety and stock of knowledge*? According to John Locke, stock *gives us freedom of thinking, as an increase of the powers and activity of the mind.*[44] The distinctive contribution of the United States to the history of liberal education has been to deploy it on behalf of the cardinal American principle: all persons have the right to pursue happiness. *Getting to know*, in Matthew Arnold's unfairly maligned phrase, *the best which has been thought and said in the world* is helpful to that free pursuit. This is sometimes scorned as elite or effete, but it is neither. Arnold makes this clear by the (seldom-quoted) phrase with which he completes his point: *and through this knowledge, turning a stream of fresh and free thought upon our stock notions and habits.*[45]

Immersion in the past helps citizens strengthen the capacity to think more clearly about the present, and better stock the future.

---

[41] *The Story of My Life* (Houghton Mifflin, 1904), 70.
[42] "Coltrane on Coltrane," *Downbeat*, September 29, 1960, 26–27.
[43] *The Merry Wives of Windsor* (2.1.56; 5.5.17).
[44] *On the Conduct of the Understanding* (1706).
[45] *Culture and Anarchy* (Smith, Elder, and Co., 1869), viii.

William Morris, design for trellis wallpaper (1862), A472. William Morris Gallery, London Borough of Waltham Forest.

12
OF CONSTRAINT

The enemy of art is the absence of limitations.
—Orson Welles

Every individual, every generation must confront aging strictures that have lost their original animating force, becoming calcified. Any manifesto, whether political or aesthetic, derives from this premise.

But it's naive to conclude that the answer to limits is limitlessness. Marlowe's Faustus and Milton's Satan share this childish drive to annihilate. Yet limitlessness becomes its own form of slackness, a damnation: *Hell hath no limits*, warns Mephistopheles. As Wendell Berry reproaches us:

> We confuse limits with confinement.... [Yet] our human and earthly limits, properly understood, are not confinements but rather inducements to formal elaboration and elegance, to *fullness* of relationship and meaning.[1]

Constraint, Berry maintains, *is not the condemnation it may seem.* Conversely, as Milton insists throughout his career, licentiousness (doing whatever you want) is not the same thing as liberty: *Thy self not free, but to thyself enthralled.*[2]

Immanuel Kant pointed out that when a dove feels the air's

---

[1] "Faustian Economics: *Hell Hath No Limits*," *Harper's Magazine*, May 2008, 38–39.
[2] The righteous Abdiel upbraiding the rebellious Lucifer, *Paradise Lost* (6.181).

resistance in flight, it *might imagine that its flight would be still easier in empty space.*[3]

No: it would drop. The resistance is what makes the lift possible. In a similar mood, Ludwig Wittgenstein envisions that we

> have got on to slippery ice where there is no friction and so in a certain sense the conditions are ideal, but also, just because of that, we are unable to walk. We want to walk: so we need *friction.* Back to the rough ground![4]

We work by having something to push off of, not by eliminating all friction. I struggle to convey this insight whenever I try to help students appreciate that formal writing—even the most basic constraint of meter—*should be thought of as the vehicle assumed by spontaneity . . . rather than as any kind of bondage.*[5]

Sometimes I point out the more obvious ways in which creation emerges because of constraint, not in spite of it: the agreed-upon time limit for a sports game, or the restricted ingredients in a cooking competition; something as banal as a project's budget and deadline; something as profound as life's finitude. There's an artistry in "making do" with what we're allotted.

Creators work within, against, and *through* constraints:

- *Perhaps giving oneself a tight structure, making limitations for oneself, squeezes out new substance where you least expect it.*

—Doris Lessing (1972)

- *Whatever diminishes constraint, diminishes strength. The more constraints one imposes, the more one frees one's self of the chains that shackle the spirit.*

—Igor Stravinsky (1939)

---

[3] *The Critique of Pure Reason* (1787), trans. Norman Kemp Smith (Macmillan, 1964), 47.

[4] *Philosophical Investigations* (1953), trans. G.E.M. Anscombe, 3rd ed. (Macmillan, 1968), sec. 107.

[5] Tamil philosopher Ananda Coomaraswamy, *The Transformation of Nature in Art* (Harvard University Press, 1934), 23.

- *The principle of limitation [is] the sole saving principle in the world. The more a person limits himself, the more resourceful he becomes.*

  —Søren Kierkegaard (1843)

- *The poetic spirit requires to be limited, that it may move within its range with a becoming liberty.*

  —A. W. Schlegel (1808)[6]

It's no paradox that constraints *enable the execution of complicated tasks.*[7] I'd extend "constraint" not just to arbitrary external impositions (like writing a fifty-thousand-word novel without the letter *e*),[8] but to the material basis of language itself. We can't write without words, which are inherited from the world and are thus "constrained." That doesn't mean language is a prison; we can still make words do things for us, in all kinds of unforeseen ways. In this sense, constraint is inevitable, and the only paradoxical thing is our unwillingness to acknowledge its pervasiveness, and *make a virtue of necessity.*[9]

Science today ratifies what poets have always known: *A person is a poet if his imagination is stimulated by the difficulties inherent in his art and not if his imagination is dulled by them.*[10] It turns out that working with limited resources induces people to be more resourceful about manipulating what they have; the key to good design is a *willingness and enthusiasm for working within these constraints.*[11]

---

[6] Lessing, preface to *The Golden Notebook* (1962; Simon and Schuster, 1971), x; Stravinsky, *Poetics of Music in the Form of Six Lessons* (1939; Harvard University Press, 1970), 65; Kierkegaard, *Either/Or*, vol. 1 (1843; Princeton University Press, 1987), 292; Schlegel, *Lectures on Dramatic Art and Literature*, trans. John Black (1808; Henry Bohn, 1846), 340.

[7] Evelyn Tribble, "Distributing Cognition in the Globe," *Shakespeare Quarterly* 56, no. 2 (2005): 135–55.

[8] A stunt that's been done! Ernest Vincent Wright, *Gadsby* (Wetzel Publishing Company, 1939).

[9] *The Two Gentlemen of Verona* (4.1.61).

[10] Paul Valéry, as paraphrased by W. H. Auden, interviewed by Michael Newman, *Paris Review* 57 (Spring 1974).

[11] Charles Eames, "What Is Design?" (1969), interviewed by Madame L'Amic, in *An*

W. H. Auden made this insight in more prayerful terms:

> Blessed be all metrical rules that forbid automatic responses,
> force us to have second thoughts, free from the fetters of Self.[12]

I love that phrase, *free from the fetters of Self*. It recalls Edmund Burke, who insisted that those who cannot govern their own appetites have *their passions forge their fetters*.[13] This inverts the juvenile fantasy that if only the Self could be free of constraint and convention, it would be liberated.

Writing and reading and discussing poetry press the *generative* nature of working within limits. Sometimes a writer falls into form, as when Elizabeth Bishop went through seventeen drafts of "One Art." The poem emerges like a butterfly from a chrysalis.[14] It began as a series of unrhymed typed sentences before discovering that *the art of losing isn't hard to master* is a refrain well-suited to the recursive mastery inherent in the villanelle form. The poem emerges from *the same kind of bottom-up, self-organizing processes seen in complex natural systems such as flocking birds, shifting sand dunes, and living trees.*[15]

At other times, we begin with the form in mind, and the work unfolds to fill its space. Consider the sonnet, as discussed in Madeleine L'Engle's *A Wrinkle in Time*:

> It is a very strict form of poetry, is it not? . . . There are fourteen lines, I believe, all in iambic pentameter. That's a very strict rhythm or meter, yes? . . . And each line has to end with a rigid rhyme pattern. And if the poet does not do it exactly this way, it is not a sonnet, is it? . . . But within this strict form the poet has complete freedom to say whatever he wants, doesn't he? . . . You're given the

---

Eames Anthology: Articles, Film Scripts, Interviews, Letters, Notes, Speeches, ed. Daniel Ostroff (Yale University Press, 2015), 285.

[12] "Shorts II," in *Collected Poems*, ed. Edward Mendelson (Vintage Books, 1991), 856.

[13] *A Letter from Mr. Burke to a Member of the National Assembly* (1791).

[14] They're held at Vassar College and have been transcribed here: https://bluedragonfly10.wordpress.com/2009/06/12/one-art-the-writing-of-loss-in-elizabeth-bishop's-poetry/.

[15] Paul Lake, "The Shape of Poetry," *Contemporary Poetry Review*, July 14, 2010.

form, but you have to write the sonnet yourself. What you say is completely up to you.[16]

What could be more arbitrary than fourteen lines! While *sonetto* at first meant a little song, with no formal limit, an Italian poet of the thirteenth century made this number of lines into a convention. That's as conventional as an 8 × 8 chessboard, or a nine-inning game, or a 3/4 waltz—yet we all play by those rules, and find ways to excel within such limits, which enable exceptional performance. If FIFA declared tomorrow that games were to last just ten minutes, or go on for two hundred, imagine the outrage from players and fans alike, as the shifted boundaries would make historical comparisons pointless. How well can you play within the frame? *That's* the game.

Because the sonnet has a 10-syllable by 14-line frame, you have a rough "budget" of 140 syllables. What happens if you go "over" budget, with 11 syllables per line (as in Shakespeare's gender-bending sonnet 20)? or 15 lines (as in his perplexing sonnet 99)? What happens if you go "under" budget, with 8 syllables per line (as in riddling sonnet 145)? or 12 lines (as in hypercoupleted sonnet 126)? These are but some of the more overt variations on the normative frame—but even the exceptions prove the rule. As A. E. Stallings admires,

> the sonnet is a form of immense versatility, flexibility, and usefulness; it is in more ways than one very Protean (in a literal, Odyssean sense—both in its changefulness and in how its true identity is paradoxically released by restriction).[17]

Rita Dove conveys the productive tension the sonnet generates: *I like how the sonnet comforts even while its prim borders (but what a*

[16] *A Wrinkle in Time* (1962; Square Fish, 2007), 219. L'Engle discusses this "structure which liberates" in *A Circle of Quiet* (Open Roads Media, 2016), 87–88.

[17] "The Catch," *Poetry* 191, no. 6 (March 2008): 474. See David Ogilvy's *Confessions of an Advertising Man* (Atheneum Books, 1963), 90: *Shakespeare wrote his sonnets within a strict discipline, fourteen lines of iambic pentameter, rhyming in three quatrains and a couplet. Were his sonnets dull?*

pretty fence!) are stultifying; one is constantly bumping up against Order.[18]

Restriction/release; order/disorder—ever since Shakespeare's era, sonneteers have played upon how sonnets *put Chaos into fourteen lines.*[19] There's even a subgenre of metasonnets about the constraints of sonnets, going back at least to the sixteenth century: *You ask a sonnet, lady, and behold! / The first line and the second are complete.*[20]

My favorite sonnet about sonnet thinking comes from William Wordsworth:

> Nuns fret not at their convent's narrow room;
> And hermits are contented with their cells;
> And students with their pensive citadels;
> Maids at the wheel, the weaver at his loom,
> Sit blithe and happy; bees that soar for bloom,
> High as the highest Peak of Furness-fells,
> Will murmur by the hour in foxglove bells:
> In truth the prison, unto which we doom
> Ourselves, no prison is: and hence for me,
> In sundry moods, 'twas pastime to be bound
> Within the Sonnet's scanty plot of ground;
> Pleased if some souls (for such there needs must be)
> Who have felt the weight of too much liberty,
> Should find brief solace there, as I have found.[21]

The first line of this scanty 10 × 14 "plot" plays off of the Italian word *stanza*—that is, "room," a place into which we bind ourselves.

---

[18] "An Intact World," in *Mother Love* (Norton, 1995), n.p.

[19] *Selected Poems of Edna St. Vincent Millay*, ed. Holly Peppe (Yale University Press, 2016), 221.

[20] *Pedes, Reyna, un Soneto, y ya le hago;*
    ya el primer verso y el segundo es hecho;
Diego Hurtado de Mendoza, *Sonnets on the Sonnet: An Anthology*, trans. Rev. Matthew Russell, SJ (Longmans, Green, and Co., 1898).

[21] *Selected Poems*, ed. John O. Hayden (Penguin Books, 1994), 174–75; *too much liberty* alludes to Claudio in *Measure for Measure* (1.2.114).

Wordsworth makes those first eight lines pause at the close of every line, whether with a semicolon, comma, or colon. Then comes a releasing enjambment—*the prison, unto which we doom / Ourselves, no prison is*—thereby enacting its own reversal of perspective: limits aren't the limits we at first believe them to be.

Sonnets abound in self-conscious reflections on freedom and constraint, with invocations of the "prison" of the form going back at least to Petrarch:

That looseth nor locketh holdeth me in prison
And holdeth me not, yet can I 'scape nowise;[22]

and continuing through today, as in these lines from Terrance Hayes:

I lock you in an American sonnet that is part prison,
Part panic closet, a little room in a house set aflame.[23]

It's one thing for me to go droning on about poetic imprisonment and autonomy in an undergraduate classroom. It's a different conversation when these poems are discussed in an actual prison. Over the past couple of years, I volunteered to teach in the West Tennessee State Penitentiary, where I was part of a faculty cohort that offers humanities seminars to incarcerated women.[24]

The program director had invited me to discuss a play, but I didn't think I could do justice to a drama in just two brief sessions. So we read Shakespeare's sonnets instead. Right choice! One student, Aja, was so enthusiastic that she came to the first class having already translated her favorite into her own verse.

[22] *Rime Sparse*, sonnet 134, translated by Sir Thomas Wyatt: https://www.poetryfounda tion.org/poems/45579/i-find-no-peace.

[23] Terrance Hayes, "American Sonnet for My Past and Future Assassin," *Poetry*, September 2017.

[24] Jonathan Rose surveys incarcerated Shakespeare programs in his compelling account *Readers' Liberation* (Oxford University Press, 2018), 112–28. Helen Wilcox suggests that the "distance" participants feel from Shakespeare might be a productive distance, something harder to obtain with contemporary work; cited in Laurence Tocci, *The Proscenium Cage: Case Studies in U.S. Theatre Prison Programs* (Cambria Press, 2007), 184. My thanks to Doug Lanier for introducing me to Wilcox's work.

The sparse classroom has a corkboard on one wall whose dimensions mirror the shape of a sonnet on the page, giving us a good visual analogue for the form: why would an artist choose to work within such a frame? G. K. Chesterton, who held that *art consists in limitation*, was only half jesting when he asserted that *the most beautiful part of every picture is the frame.*[25]

It's a cliché, but a true cliché: with no papers, no tests, no grades, no administrators (and no broken classroom technology!), this was the rawest, most inspired education I've experienced, corroborating John Berger's Hamlet-like belief that because *the prison is now as large as the planet. . . . Liberty is slowly being found not outside but in the depths of the prison.*[26] The students want to be there: over fifty had applied for just fifteen spots. Those enrolled wrote us effusive introductory notes:

> *I love to learn new things.* (Nancy)
> *I love to learn. I feel I can never have enough knowledge.* (Kimberly)
> *I love to learn and feel it is important to continue to grow.* (Denice)

They let out a joyful whoop after reciting these words:

> Stone Walls do not a Prison make,
>   Nor Iron bars a Cage;
> Minds innocent and quiet take
>   That for an Hermitage.
> If I have freedom in my Love,
>   And in my soul am free,
> Angels alone that soar above,
>   Enjoy such Liberty.[27]

While instructors aren't told students' sentences, I'm aware that some individuals will be confined there for life, making a medita-

[25] Cited by Ian Ker, *Chesterton: A Biography* (Oxford University Press, 2012), 254.
[26] John Berger, "Fellow Prisoners," *Guernica Magazine*, July 15, 2011.
To me [Denmark] is a prison.
Hamlet (2.2.231.11–12).
[27] The final stanza of Richard Lovelace's "To Althea, from Prison," in *Lucasta* (1649), 98.

tion on the soul's "Liberty" all the more visceral. (Lovelace's own comparatively brief imprisonment—for seven weeks in 1642—looks rather less daunting in contrast.) They thanked me at the end of each session, shaking my hand upon departure (something no other class has done in two decades of teaching).

We pondered a perennial task: how can an artist revivify a tired genre, without abandoning it? By the time Shakespeare composed his sonnets, the form had already fallen out of fashion ("that's so fifteen-ninety-*late*!"). To bring it back to life, he modified the conventional male speaker idealizing female addressee into a fresh configuration: an older man chiding a younger intimate. And he then modified his *own* modified pattern, with sonnets 127–54 a lust-and-jealousy-fueled subset, addressed to a woman.

Poets ceaselessly renew forms. Take Jericho Brown's "The Tradition,"[28] where the innocuous-looking title turns embittered by the close:

Aster. Nasturtium. Delphinium. We thought
Fingers in dirt meant it was our dirt, learning
Names in heat, in elements classical
Philosophers said could change us. *Star Gazer.*
Foxglove. Summer seemed to bloom against the will
Of the sun, which news reports claimed flamed hotter
On this planet than when our dead fathers
Wiped sweat from their necks. *Cosmos. Baby's Breath.*
Men like me and my brothers filmed what we
Planted for proof we existed before
Too late, sped the video to see blossoms
Brought in seconds, colors you expect in poems
Where the world ends, everything cut down.
John Crawford. Eric Garner. Mike Brown.

[28] Jericho Brown, "The Tradition," from *The Tradition.* Copyright © 2019 by Jericho Brown. Reprinted with the permission of The Permissions Company, LLC on behalf of Copper Canyon Press: www.coppercanyonpress.org. Reproduced with permission of the Pan Macmillan through PLSclear.

Brown opens by naming flowers—a tender, familiar gesture in Renaissance verse, from Edmund Spenser's *Sweete Marioram, and Daysies decking prime* to Shakespeare's *oxlips and the nodding violet*, from John Milton's mournful *ground with vernal flowers* to Hester Pulter's *tulip, rose, or gillyflower*.[29] Yet, by the end of the poem, naming turns into memorializing *blossoms . . . cut down*—black victims of police brutality.

"The Tradition" evokes everything from the tradition of poetic form, to the tradition of treating poems as "posies" ("anthology" even comes from the Greek words *anthos* "flowers" + *legein* "to gather"), to the miserable "tradition" of American violence, handed down from generation to generation. In interviews, Brown relates how he began the poem without anticipating how it would conclude, yet *our form informs our content . . . they go back and forth with one another . . . they're having a conversation*.[30] Part of that conversation takes place within the poet; part of it involves the writer's world-historical moment; and part of it unfolds across time. As Brown avers, *Certainly, I would not have been able to write my poems if Donne had not existed*.[31]

How can we, as readers, read ourselves into dead poets from distant nations and ages? Shakespeare's work has proved to be malleable across centuries, peoples, and languages. As Maya Angelou provocatively claimed about sonnet 29 (*I all alone beweep my outcast state*):

Of course he wrote it for me; that is a condition of the black woman. Of course, he was a black woman. I understand that. No-

[29] Spenser, *Muiopotmos, or the Fate of the Butterflie*, line 192, in *Edmund Spenser: The Shorter Poems*, ed. Richard A. McCabe (Penguin Books, 1999); Shakespeare, *A Midsummer Night's Dream* (2.1.250); Milton, *Lycidas*, line 141; Pulter, "View But this Tulip" (Emblem 40, line 1). See Frances Dolan's helpful mapping, "Posies: The Flower/Writing Connection," in *The Pulter Project: Poet in the Making*, ed. Leah Knight and Wendy Wall (2018): http://pulterproject.northwestern.edu.

[30] Jericho Brown, in conversation with Michael Dumanis, *Bennington Review*, October 27, 2018: http://www.benningtonreview.org/jericho-brown-interview.

[31] Jericho Brown interview, *Lightbox Poetry*, January 6, 2016: http://lightboxpoetry.com/?p=516.

body else understands it, but I know that William Shakespeare was a black woman.[32]

Shortly before she died, she universalized this claim: *[His] poetry . . . has been written for you, each of you—black, white, Hispanic, man, woman, gay, straight.*[33]

My students at the penitentiary didn't need convincing, but this sentiment never felt truer for me.

[32] "The Role of Art in Life," *Connections Quarterly*, September 1985, 14, 28.
[33] Karen Swallow Prior, "What Maya Angelou Means When She Says 'Shakespeare Must Be a Black Girl,' " *Atlantic*, January 30, 2013.

Visual alphabet, from Johannes Host von Romberch's *Congestorium Artificiose Memorie* (1533). Rare Book Division, The New York Public Library.

13

OF MAKING

Word-work is sublime, she thinks, because it is generative.
—Toni Morrison, Nobel Lecture (1993)

Make magazine launched in February 2005 by proclaiming *Some of us are born <u>makers</u> and others, like me, become <u>makers</u> almost without realizing it,*[1] an echo of the line *Some are born great, some achieve greatness, and some have greatness thrust upon 'em,* from *Twelfth Night* (2.5.126–28).

The first Maker Faire followed in 2006, a phenomenon that's since spread worldwide. We now have public libraries offering "makerspaces" for patrons to tinker with technology, and educational policy mavens championing "maker-centered learning," where project-based inquiry blends a DIY ethos with good old-fashioned learning-by-doing. The maker movement has been thrust upon us. All such approaches derive from the premise that making is a form of thinking. In John Ruskin's chiasmus, *The workman ought often to be thinking, and the thinker often to be working.*[2]

Unfortunately, there are gaps in the self-awareness of the maker movement, which acts as if this is *new*; it's *revolutionary*; it's *never been done before.* A little historical modesty is in order: Victor

---

[1] Dale Dougherty, "The Making of *Make,*" *Make: Technology on Your Time*, February 2005, 7.
[2] "The Nature of Gothic," in *The Stones of Venice: Volume the Third. The Fall* (Smith, Elder, and Co., 1853), 169.

Della-Vos's method of manual instruction dates back to the 1860s; John Dewey's Lab School began promulgating "learning by doing" over a century ago.[3] We could point to many earlier historical "makespheres" where hands-on education unfolded, including the "maker's knowledge" traditions of early modern artisanal workshops, where making was bound to knowing. And the purported novelty of the maker movement is often blind to communities where making has been a long-standing necessity, not just a hobby:

> If you can't afford clothes, but you can make them—make them. You have to work with what you have, especially if you don't have a lot of money. You use creativity, and you use imagination.[4]

And there's a yet deeper flaw: the presumption that "making" ought to be STEM-driven, comprehending only physical objects.

But don't we make things out of words, too?

A century ago, George Cram Cook knew better when he offered the first creative writing course, which he called "Verse Making."[5] Today's burgeoning creative writing programs found their genesis not with the goal of publishing in mind, but rather a deeper appreciation of the architecture of writing from the inside:

> It was an effort on their part to bring the teaching of literature more closely in line with the ways in which (they believed) literature is genuinely created.... They sought to impart the *understanding* of literature through the *use* of it.[6]

---

[3] Harvey Alvy, *Fighting for Change in Your School* (ACSD, 2017), 120.

[4] Edwidge Danticat, "All Immigrants Are Artists," in *Light the Dark*, ed. Joe Fassler (Penguin, 2017), 95.

[5] John C. Gerber, "The Emergence of the Writers' Workshop," in *A Community of Writers*, ed. Robert Dana (University of Iowa Press, 1999), 225.

[6] D. G. Myers, *The Elephants Teach* (University of Chicago Press, 1996), 4, 6.

Tudor educators relied on what they called "unmaking": breaking down passages and words in order to see how they were assembled. John Brinsley lauded

> resolving and unmaking the Latine of the Author, and then making it againe just after the same manner, as it was unmade.[7]

We unmake, in order to remake, and make something our own. *If a poet is anybody*, wrote E. E. Cummings, it's *somebody who is obsessed by Making*.[8]

Writers recur to the parallels between wordcraft and other modes of making, as when Sandra Maria Esteves calls the poet's eye *an architect's pen . . . a carpenter's knife edged in rays of light*.[9] Yusef Komunyakaa meditates on the affinity between his father's work as a carpenter and his own as a writer:

> Isn't that how we poets make poems? We measure the music of a line. We shape. We cut. We revise. We re-see. Even the improvisational verse is worked, polished, finished. It becomes. As a grown man at times, in a reverie, I am still five trying to hold a plank as my father saws. Through the hands, memory awakens, and it is here in the body that poetry and carpentry are inherently connected.[10]

He cites a passage from Pablo Neruda's "Ars Poetica (1)":

> Then I cut into the board
> of my choice
> with the sputtering points of my saw:

---

[7] Cited in Jeff Dolven, *Scenes of Instruction* (University of Chicago Press, 2007), 37.

[8] Cited by Robert Graves in "The Making of the Poem," in *The Common Asphodel* (Haskell House, 1949), 117.

[9] "There Is a Poet Inside You," in *Bluestown Mockingbird Mambo* (Arte Publico Press, 1990), 37.

[10] "Honor Thy Hands: Carpentry and Poetry," *American Reader* 1, no. 4 (February/March 2013): http://theamericanreader.com/honor-thy-hands-carpentry-and-poetry/.

from the plank come my verses,
like chips freed from the block,
sweet-smelling, swarthy, remote,
while the poem lays down its deck
and its hull, calculates list,
lifts up its bulk by the road
and the ocean inhabits it.[11]

Neruda calls up two senses of "craft": that of a seaworthy vessel, and that of the cumulative practices, refined through experience and in response to material.

Writer as architect, writer as carpenter, sculptor, weaver, gardener, builder—these are recurrent figures of the *making* embraced in verbal creation. Our digital "cutting and pasting" is itself a residue from the physical excising and adhering practices of earlier eras. And our word "fiction" derives from the Latin for *shaping, devising*, in turn going back to Proto-Indo-European roots like *dheigh* "to form, build"; *dhe* "to set, put"; and *dhabh-* "to fit together."[12]

In the thirteenth century, Geoffrey of Vinsauf made the link between architectural thinking and verbal creation overt:

The mind's hand shapes the entire house before the body's hand builds it. Its mode of being is archetypal before it is actual. Poetic art may see in this analogy the law to be given to poets: . . . As a prudent workman, construct the whole fabric within the mind's citadel; let it exist in the mind before it is on the lips.[13]

---

[11] Excerpt from *World's End* (*Fin de mundo*), © Pablo Neruda, 1969, y Fundación Pablo Neruda. *Five Decades: Poems 1925–1970*, copyright © 1974 by Grove Press, Inc. Used by permission of Grove/Atlantic, Inc. Any third party use of this material, outside of this publication, is prohibited.

[12] See the ever-expanding work of Douglas Harper's *Online Etymology Dictionary*: https://www.etymonline.com.

[13] *Poetria Nova* (c. 1210).

In this, he was following Pindar, one of the oldest extant Greek poets: *Raising the fine-walled porch of our dwelling with golden pillars, we will build, as it were, a marvelous hall.*[14] The foundational link between lyric and construction was made literal by the mythical Amphion, whose lyre was reputed to have helped build the walls of Thebes. Now that's *making*.

It's telling that the Greek verb for "making" or "doing" was *poiein*—the same word that gives us "poet." Aristotle discussed *poesis* in both his treatise on ethics and his treatise on drama; both probe the appropriate forms of making. It is in this sense that Auden proclaims the artist to be *a maker, a fabricator of objects.*[15]

This etymology of *poet* appeals because it speaks to *the very simple notion of making . . . <u>works of the mind</u>, that is to say, those works which the mind decides to make for its own use, employing in the process all the physical means at its disposal.*[16] Aldous Huxley reminds us:

> The poet is, etymologically, the maker. Like all makers, he requires a stock of raw materials—in his case, experience. Experience is a matter of sensibility and intuition, of seeing and hearing significant things, of paying attention at the right moments, of understanding and coordinating. Experience is not what happens to a man; it is what a man does with what happens to him. It is a gift for dealing with the accidents of existence, not the accidents themselves.[17]

As early as the fourteenth century, English poets were called "makers," with Chaucer praised by his peer Thomas Usk for how his *wit*

[14] *Olympian* 6, trans. Diane Arnson Svarlien (1990), Project Perseus: http://www.perseus.tufts.edu/hopper/text?doc=Perseus%3Atext%3A1999.01.0162%3Abook%3DO.%3Apoem%3D6.

[15] *Secondary Worlds* (Random House, 1968), 141.

[16] *The Collected Works of Paul Valéry: Aesthetics*, trans. R. Manheim (Princeton University Press, 1971), 91–92.

[17] *Texts & Pretexts: An Anthology with Commentaries* (Chatto & Windus, 1933), 5.

and ... good reason of sentence ... passeth al other makers.[18] As late as 1772, one could lament that England no longer produced *true makers* like Spenser and Sidney—both of whom appealed to the Greek etymology of *poesis* in their work.[19] Making was both divine (akin to the acts of the Maker) and mortal (a worker's struggles with material).

What are those materials? To which previous artists are they responding? How is their work a product of their time? How have they made something out of bits and pieces of other sources, other traditions, other media? And how can we revive this sense of *making* in our world—acting as thinkers, not mere consumers?

All kinds of "makers" pervade Shakespeare's plays:

> noisemakers, grave-makers, jig-makers, hornmakers, peacemakers, ballad-makers, ropemakers, gallows-makers, shoemakers, cuckold-makers, card-makers, widow-makers, sailmakers, and makers of manners.[20]

In *Hamlet*, the grave-makers exchange this jest about the endurance of different kinds of making:

> GRAVEDIGGER. What is he that builds stronger than either the mason, the shipwright, or the carpenter?
> SECOND MAN. The gallowsmaker, for that outlives a thousand tenants.[21]

My students' papers often describe Shakespeare as a play-*write*: they hear the homophone for what they presume a playwright does: *write*. But it's spelled *w-r-i-g-h-t*, from the Anglo-Saxon

---

[18] *Testament of Love*, ed. Gary W. Shawver (University of Toronto Press, 2002), 160.

[19] *Verses prefixed to Browne's Pastorals.* Spenser, E.K.'s Glossary to "April," in *Shepherd's Calendar* (1579); Sidney, *An Apologie for Poetry* (1595).

[20] Corinne Viglietta, "What's Shakespeare Got to Do with the Maker Movement?" Folger Shakespeare Library: https://folgereducation.wordpress.com/2015/01/27/whats-shakespeare-got-to-do-with-the-maker-movement/.

[21] *Hamlet* (5.1.35–38).

wryhta, glossed in 1567 by Laurence Nowell's Saxon dictionary as "A woorkman, a wright, a common name of all artificers … a poet"[22]—like a cartwright, who crafts carts, or a shipwright, who crafts ships. There were arkwrights, battle-wrights, boatwrights, bread-wrights, butterwrights, candlewrights, millwrights, wain-wrights. A playwright crafts plays. They are *wrought*—designed, molded, fabricated, formed, contorted, sharpened, bent, formed, polished.

In praising the poet as having a skill to create that veers toward divinity (the "Heavenly Maker of that maker") Sidney follows Landino's commentary on Dante's *Comedia* (1481):

> The Greeks say 'poet' from the verb '*poiein*': which is halfway be-tween 'creating' (*creare*), which is proper to God when he brought everything into being from out of nothing: and 'making' (*fare*) which is proper to men when in each art, they compose from ma-terial and form. For this reason, although the poet's figment is not entirely out of nothing, yet he departs from making and ap-proaches quite near to creating. And God is a poet, and the world his poem.[23]

Scaliger, Tasso, and others concurred: *There is no one in the world who deserves the name of Creator but God and the Poet.*[24]

Against this audacious comparison, Auden countered: *poetry makes nothing happen.*[25]

What a bleak evaluation! one that sanctions every hostile sus-picion about the frivolity of reading. It's a good corrective to the stridency of Percy Bysshe Shelley's *poets are the unacknowledged*

[22] Found via the *Lexicons of Early Modern English (LEME)*: https://leme.library.utoronto.ca.

[23] Translated by Rachel Porcher, in "The Word, the Workman, and the World" (MA thesis, University of London, 2015), 2.

[24] Graham Wallas, citing Percy Bysshe Shelley, citing Tasso, *The Art of Thought* (1926; Solis Press, 2014), 69.

[25] "In Memory of W. B. Yeats," in *Another Time* (Random House, 1940), 93–96.

legislators of the world[26]—the consolation being that the world *does* run by the laws of artists, it just doesn't *know* it.

But reconsider the phrasing of Auden's line *poetry makes nothing happen*. There's a more negative way in which this *might* have been put: *Poetry does not make anything happen*. In contrast, this line makes the positive declaration: *poetry makes*. Think of the phrase without the word "nothing" in it: *Poetry makes_____ happen*. There is a way to read this absence as a kind of presence. How *can* you make "a nothing" happen? In the following lines, Auden imagines poetry as *a way of happening*, one that *survives / In the valley of its making*.

Aristotle suggested that the function of the *maker's mind* resembled the revealing function of light, which does not *cause* vision, but helps make vision possible.[27] In this sense, Coriolanus's defiant attempt to be *author of himself* can be seen in a more creative light, *Myself must I remake*.[28] There's a reciprocal process of self-shaping that emerges in the process of making, as when Comenius insisted, *Thus, by good practice, all will at last feel the truth of the proverb: fabricando fabricamur [By creating, we create ourselves]*.[29]

The German word *Bildung* gets at this sense of educational *making*, inviting the (etymologically wrong, but still poetically correct!) connection to *building*. Or perhaps the better English analogue is *edification*, a favorite term of sixteenth-century teachers for what they were making through their students. Taylor Mali's poem "What Teachers Make" responds to the rude query

[26] *A Defence of Poetry* (composed 1821; published 1840), in Percy Bysshe Shelley, *The Major Works*, ed. Zachary Leader and Michael O'Neill (Oxford University Press, 2003), 674–701.

[27] L. A. Kosman, "What Does the Maker's Mind Make?" in *Essays on Aristotle's "De Anima"*, ed. Martha Nussbaum and Amelie Rorty (Oxford University Press, 1992), 343–58.

[28] *Coriolanus* (5.3.36); "An Acre of Grass," in *Collected Poems of W. B. Yeats*, ed. Richard J. Finneran (Macmillan, 1996), 332.

[29] Pierre Bovet, *Jean Amos Comenius* (Geneva, 1943), 23.

("What do you make?"—as in: *how much money*) by doubling down on the *makerly* aspects of teaching: *Teachers make a goddamn difference! Now what about you?*[30]

Education is the place where the nothing that means everything happens, in letting us participate in the general art of Making, *the mirror in which we see ourselves.*[31]

[30] *What Learning Leaves* (Hanover Press, 2002).
[31] Frank Bidart, "Advice to the Players," in *Music like Dirt* (Sarabande Books, 2002), 14.

Allan Warren, James Baldwin with a statue of William Shakespeare, 1969. Courtesy of Allan Warren/CC BY-SA 3.0.

14
OF FREEDOM

Only one study truly deserves the name
"liberal": that which makes a person free.
—Seneca, Letter 88 to Lucilius (c. 65 CE)

We don't know much about the great Greek fabulist Aesop. He may have even been a fable himself! Whether he lived or whether he was instead a fictive composite character, my favorite event in his (presumed) biography is how he earned his freedom from slavery—on account of his storytelling. His stories became staples of educators for centuries, from the *Progymnasmata* to John Locke. Like folk traditions around the globe, they include talking animals, whose voices uncannily resemble our own.

In one Aesopian fable, a plain bird (often a crow) adorns itself in the plumage of others. Schoolmaster John Brinsley offered two popular versions in 1617:

> A Chough of a time tricked up himself with the feathers of a peacock. And then seeming to himself very gay, disdaining his own kind, he betook himself to the company of the peacocks. They at length understanding the deceit, stript the foolish bird of his colors, and whipped him.

> this little fable of a jackdaw . . . being trimmed with feathers which she had gathered together, which had fallen from other birds, after that every one of the birds pluckt again her own feather, became ridiculous.[1]

---

[1] *Esops Eables [sic] translated grammatically* (1617), 20.

Brinsley concludes with the Socratic injunction *Know thyself.* (When reading these stories to my children, I've often found the "moral" lessons appended are more pat than clarifying!)

Sir Roger L'Estrange's version elaborates:

> We steal from one another in all manner of Ways, and to all manner of Purposes; Wit, as well as Feathers; but where Pride and Beggary meet, People are sure to be made Ridiculous in the Conclusion.[2]

Most morals to this fable concur that the vain imposter was justly punished for his pretensions. But I wonder. Aesop is nothing if not a gatherer and adapter of others' stories; might not he be somewhat fond of this plucky bird?

The first mention of Shakespeare's career alludes to Aesop. It appears in a scornful 1592 pamphlet, warning university-trained playwrights not to share their work with an

> upstart crow, beautified with our feathers, that with his *tiger's heart wrapped in a player's hide*, supposes he is as well able to bombast out a blank verse as the best of you: and being an absolute *Johannes factotum*, is in his own conceit the only Shake-scene in a country.[3]

Throwing shade on a line from this *Shake-scene: O tiger's heart wrapped in a woman's hide!*[4]

What irks Robert Greene is the presumptuousness of this *upstart*, borrowing *our feathers*, who *supposes* he is as good as *the best* of us, *in his own conceit*. Yet Shakespeare had the last word, as his wondrous late play *The Winter's Tale* lifts from Greene's *Pandosto*

---

[2] *Fables of Æsop and Other Eminent Mythologists* (1669), 32.

[3] *Greenes, groats-vvorth of witte, bought with a million of repentance.* This, and other primary-source materials related to Shakespeare's life, can be found scanned in the Folger Shakespeare Library's *Shakespeare Documented* collection: https://shakespearedocumented.folger.edu/exhibition/document/greenes-groats-worth-witte-first-printed-allusion-shakespeare-playwright.

[4] *3 Henry VI* (1.4.137).

and includes the unrepentant thief Autolycus, *a snapper-up of unconsidered trifles* (4.3.25–26). Shake *that* scene.

An aspiring young performer, not from around here (recent transplant from the sticks, with limited education), trying to sound like us . . . *who does he think he is?* His peers "reacted with jealousy, contempt and ridicule" to this "literary magpie"—I mean, Bob Dylan.[5] Fans have long chronicled the Shakespearean echoes across his career, whether nodding to play titles (*Tempest*), characters (Ophelia in "Desolation Row"), phrases ("Time out of mind," from Mercutio's Queen Mab speech), or more general inspiration ("I've been trying for years to come up with songs that have the feeling of a Shakespearean drama").[6]

Dylan and Shakespeare have even shared the occasional rhyme. Citing the first quatrain of Shakespeare's sonnet 138 and Dylan's "Something There Is about You," Christopher Ricks notes how

> rhymes for *truth* are few . . . perhaps the only word into metaphorical relation with which a rhyme can creatively bring *truth* [is] the word *youth*. . . . [Dylan] deftly supplements his rhyme of *youth* and *truth* with the names of *Ruth* and *Duluth*.[7]

Even more telling have been Dylan's recent invocations of Shakespeare's artistic process, in defense of the poet's freedom to create from any source whatsoever. In response to 2012 accusations of plagiarism, Dylan reminded an interviewer that similar charges had dogged him since 1963—*if you think it's so easy to quote . . . do it yourself and see how far you can get*[8]—recalling Virgil's response to charges that he had plagiarized Homer: *And why don't they try the same thefts? They would soon understand that it's easier to pinch*

[5] Robert Shelton, *Bob Dylan: No Direction Home* (Omnibus, 2011), 197; Susan Tomaselli, cited by Martin Doyle, "Bob Dylan's Nobel Prize Divides Irish Writers and Literary Critics," *Irish Times*, October 13, 2016.

[6] Robert Love, Bob Dylan interview, *Independent*, February 7, 2015.

[7] "Lies," in *The Force of Poetry* (Clarendon Press, 1984), 375.

[8] Interview with Mikal Gilmore, "Bob Dylan Unleashed," *Rolling Stone*, September 27, 2012.

Hercules' club than a line from Homer.[9] As Woody Guthrie once said of another songwriter: *Aw, he just stole from me, but I steal from everybody.*[10]

Dylan insists, *quotation is a rich and enriching tradition . . . It goes way back . . . you make it yours.*[11] You make it *yours.* Dylan later divulges:

> These songs of mine, they're like mystery stories, the kind that Shakespeare saw when he was growing up. I think you could trace what I do back that far. . . . These songs didn't come out of thin air. . . . It all came out of traditional music.[12]

This is how to transcend the squawking about "our feathers"—by noting how one tunes in to the past, dials in to a tradition. Dylan elsewhere recounts late-night radio:

> I remember listening to the Staple Singers' "Uncloudy Day." And it was the most mysterious thing I'd ever heard. It was like the fog rolling in. What was that? How do you make that? . . . I felt that life itself was a mystery.[13]

As someone who grew up in Dylan's Duluth and now resides in Mavis's Memphis, I love that idea of the Staples' voices reaching him across the airwaves, all the way from the Delta to the top of Highway 61.

That word "mystery" recurs, referring not only to something *mysterious*, but also to *craft*, in the sense of the arcane knowledge ("mystery") the medieval guilds would have transmitted between master and apprentice—senses that converged when those same

---

[9] As reported by Donatus in *The Life of Virgil*, trans. D. A. Russell, *Criticism in Antiquity* (University of California Press, 1981), 189.

[10] Related by Pete Seeger, "Johnny Appleseed, Jr.," *Sing Out* 23 (1974): 22.

[11] Interview with Mikal Gilmore, "Bob Dylan Unleashed."

[12] Randall Roberts, "Grammys 2015: Transcript of Bob Dylan's MusiCares Person of Year Speech," *Los Angeles Times*, February 7, 2015.

[13] Robert Love, "Bob Dylan: The Uncut Interview," *AARP The Magazine*, February/March 2015; reprinted in Jeff Burger, *Dylan on Dylan: Interviews and Encounters* (Chicago Review Press, 2018), 350.

craft guilds performed religious plays. And that word *make* recurs as well: *How do you make that? You make it yours.*

That Shakespearean sense *of mine own making* permeates his Nobel acceptance speech as well:

> When he was writing *Hamlet*, I'm sure he was thinking about a lot of different things: "Who're the right actors for these roles?" "How should this be staged?" "Do I really want to set this in Denmark?" His creative vision and ambitions were no doubt at the forefront of his mind, but there were also more mundane matters to consider and deal with. "Is the financing in place?" "Are there enough good seats for my patrons?" "Where am I going to get a human skull?" . . . like Shakespeare, I too am often occupied with the pursuit of my creative endeavors and dealing with all aspects of life's mundane matters. "Who are the best musicians for these songs?" "Am I recording in the right studio?" "Is this song in the right key?" Some things never change, even in 400 years.[14]

(This speech is another instance of Dylan's "love and theft"—some of it seems to have been cribbed from SparkNotes!)

There's nothing *innate* about a Jewish kid from northern Minnesota tuning in to a gospel family from the segregated south, just as there was nothing innate about a Warwickshire lad tuning in to distant peoples and distant times, nor was there anything innate about a lamed Greek slave plucking stories and making them his own. As Terence, another ex-slave freed by his wit, has one of his characters proclaim, *I am human: nothing human is alien to me.*[15]

James Baldwin's writing charted the oscillation between alienation and ownership. In the autobiographical note that precedes

---

[14] *2 Henry IV* (Epilogue.4). Or, from *The Phoenix and the Turtle*: "Either was the other's mine" (36). Bob Dylan, Nobel Banquet speech (December 10, 2016): https://www.nobelprize.org/nobel_prizes/literature/laureates/2016/dylan-speech_en.html.

[15] *Heauton Timorumenos* (The Self-Tormentor). Anthony Appiah calls Terence's line "something like the golden rule of cosmopolitanism." *Cosmopolitanism: Ethics in a World of Strangers* (Norton, 2007), 111.

Notes of a Native Son, he confided that he initially *brought to Shakespeare . . . a special attitude*:

> These were not really my creations, they did not contain my history; I might search in them in vain forever for any reflection of myself. I was an interloper; this was not my heritage.[16]

Yet he then pivots: *I would have to appropriate these white centuries, I would have to make them mine.*

There's that language of *making mine* again. In an edition revised decades later, Baldwin reiterates, even more forcefully:

> I had to claim my birthright. I am what time, circumstance, history, have made of me, certainly, but I am, also, much more than that. So are we all.[17]

So are we all. While Baldwin's exclusions were more brutally pervasive than Dylan's or Shakespeare's ever were, the refrain's the same: becoming *the heir of a cultural birthright.*[18]

This sense of earning our—*your*—common cultural stock goes back through Seneca (*The best ideas are common property . . . whatever is well said by anyone is mine*) to Isocrates (*The deeds of the past are . . . an inheritance common to us all*).[19] You belong here: you can *sit with Shakespeare and he winces not.*[20]

---

[16] *Notes of a Native Son* (Beacon Press, 1955), 10.

[17] (Beacon Press, 1984), xii.

[18] Wendell Berry, *The Unsettling of America: Culture and Agriculture* (Random House, 1977), 157.

[19] Seneca, *Ad Lucilium epistulae morales: Books I–LXI*, trans. Richard M. Gummere (William Heinemann, 1917), 73, 107; Isocrates, *Panegyricus*, trans. George Norlin (Loeb Classical Library, 1930), 9.

[20] W.E.B. Du Bois, *The Souls of Black Folk* (1903), ed. Henry Louis Gates, Jr. (Oxford University Press, 2014), 80. As W. Somerset Maugham rightly insists:

> The best homage we can pay to the great figures of the past, Dante, Titian, Shakespeare, Spinoza, is to treat them not with reverence, but with the familiarity we should exercise if they were our contemporaries. Thus we pay them the highest compliment we can; our familiarity acknowledges that they are alive for us.

The Summing Up (1938; William Heinemann, 1954), 271.

Think back to Greene's denigration of Shakespeare as "upstart crow." The claim wasn't only that Shakespeare was like an animal, mimicking ("parroting"); the point was that he didn't even have a *right* to these words and this activity.

An essay Baldwin composed for the four hundredth anniversary of Shakespeare's birth captures this dynamic from the moment you read its title: "Why I Stopped Hating Shakespeare."[21] Recalling how as a youth he resented Shakespeare as a *chauvinist*—indeed condemning him as *one of the authors and architects of my oppression*—Baldwin realized that he *missed the point entirely*. He recognized that his resistance to Shakespeare was a resistance to English itself. It was Baldwin's time in France that *forced me into a new relationship* with his own language. (Double translation at work again!)

> My quarrel with the English language has been that the language reflected none of my experience. But now I began to see the matter in quite another way. If the language was not my own, it might be the fault of the language; but it might also be my fault. Perhaps the language was not my own because I had never attempted to use it, had only learned to imitate it.

Baldwin saw that he must move beyond the necessary but early stage of imitation, to the stage that makes that external voice internal, synthesizing it into one's own . . . ultimately, an act of freedom. This sense of responsibility—*responsiveness, responding*—to Shakespeare emerges in concert with Baldwin's reflection on the blues, jazz, and the sorrow songs:

> The authority of this language was in its candor, its irony, its density, and its beat: this was the authority of the language which produced me, and it was also the authority of Shakespeare.

[21] *The Cross of Redemption*, ed. Randall Kenan (Vintage, 2010). Baldwin's essay can be found online: http://aalbc.com/authors/why_i_stopped_hating_shakespeare.html.

With lacerating insight, Baldwin concludes: *My relationship, then, to the language of Shakespeare revealed itself as nothing less than my relationship to myself and my past.*

There's a classic political distinction between negative liberty and positive liberty. It's the difference between "freedom from" (as in, *I am slave to no man*) and "freedom to" (as in, *I am my own master*).[22] At first, Baldwin sought freedom *from* having to read Shakespeare; yet he came to relish the freedom *to* make Shakespeare his own. In doing so, Baldwin achieved a mutual recognition in Shakespeare that few of us ever reach—*an inner freedom which cannot be attained in any other way* than through inhabiting other minds through art.[23]

Today both "liberal" and "arts" suffer from narrow connotations that don't convey the vital ambitions of this program of study. "Liberal" is now wrongly conflated with a leftist political stance; "arts" are presumed to be nothing more than various forms of creative studio work (which I hasten to add *are* part of the liberal arts, if often maligned). A former college president recounts the dismaying results of focus groups, where nineteen out of twenty parents

> agreed that liberal arts referred to either studying soft, "touchy feely" subjects, like psychology as opposed to physics, or studying something "leftish" that "came out of the 60s." Ouch.[24]

But "liberal" just meant "free," and "arts" meant something far more comprehensive, like science, or knowledge, or craft. The emancipatory *artes liberales* were *crafts of freedom*: the highest level of think-

---

[22] Isaiah Berlin, "Two Concepts of Liberty," in *Four Essays On Liberty* (1958; Oxford University Press, 1969), 118–72.

[23] Ernst Cassirer, *An Essay on Man* (Doubleday & Co., 1953), 149; discussed by Geoffrey Galt Harpham in *What Do You Think, Mr. Ramirez? The American Revolution in Education* (University of Chicago Press, 2017), 34–35.

[24] John Strassburger, "For the Liberal Arts, Rhetoric Is Not Enough," *Chronicle of Higher Education*, February 28, 2010. (There's that dismissal of "rhetoric," yet once more!)

ing suitable to a free citizen—*the bane of every despot.*[25] Such an educational program presumes that freedom is fragile, demanding vigilant, endless exertion: *there is nothing more arduous than the apprenticeship of liberty.*[26]

While the liberal arts were distinguished from the manual skills required for practical labor, conducted by the uneducated and the disenfranchised (often slaves and women), *crafts of freedom* embrace any practice (whether physical or intellectual) that emancipates us from what Blake called *mind-forg'd manacles.*[27] As bell hooks reminds us, the classroom is where we can *labor for freedom . . . This is education as the practice of freedom.*[28]

When Caliban cries out for freedom, he falls for a drunk Stephano, who sings, *Thought is free.*[29] This phrase *embodies one of the dramatist's most daring and schematic ironies.*[30] At this precise moment, Caliban's *not* free—he's just transferred his slavery to *a new master.* Real freedom would demand not only being slave to no man, but being his own master.

Here are some undertones of that phrase:

"thought is free"; speech isn't.

"thought is free"—so they say.

"thought is free" to wander as it will.

"thought is free," as is thoughtlessness.

"thought is free," so long as you earn it.

"thought is free," but true liberty is laborious.

"thought is free," once you remove obstacles to thinking.

"thought is free," yet it requires infrastructure to achieve that freedom.

---

[25] Hamza Yusuf, "The Liberal Arts in an Illiberal Age: Freeing Thought from the Shackles of Feeling and Desire," *Renovatio: The Journal of Zaytuna College*, December 18, 2018.

[26] Alexis de Tocqueville, *Democracy in America*, vol. 1 (1835; Vintage Books, 1960), 256.

[27] "London," in *Songs of Innocence and Experience* (1794): https://www.bl.uk/romantics-and-victorians/articles/looking-at-the-manuscript-of-william-blakes-london.

[28] *Teaching to Transgress* (Routledge, 1994), 207.

[29] *The Tempest* (3.2.116).

[30] John Berryman, *The Freedom of the Poet* (Farrar, Straus and Giroux, 1976), 81.

Thought is free was proverbial, dating back to Cicero; Shakespeare himself had already cited it.[31] It appears in the first poem written by King James: *Since thought is free, think what thou will.*[32] Spanish educator Juan Luis Vives upheld it as a motto:

> Thought is free. Who will produce thought by force? The power of truth . . . All men are equal.[33]

Even this one curt proverb demonstrates how the craft of intellectual freedom emerges through an ongoing conversation with past thinkers—in Martin Luther King Jr.'s resonant phrase, *going forward by going backward.*[34]

King was a lifelong remaker of Shakespeare, most memorably in his "I Have a Dream" speech: *this sweltering summer of the Negro's legitimate discontent.*[35] King knew better than anyone that

> thinking critically means that the individual must think imaginatively, creatively, originally. Originality is a basic part of education. That does not mean that you think something altogether new; if that were the case Shakespeare wasn't original, for Shakespeare depended on Plutarch and others for many of his plots. Originality does not mean thinking up something totally new in the universe, but it does mean giving new validity to old form.[36]

Giving new validity to old form—that's the kind of Shakespearean spirit we need. Education ought to exercise us in the crafts of free-

---

[31] *Twelfth Night* (1.3.63). See Morris Palmer Tilley, *Elizabethan Proverb Lore* (Macmillan & Company, 1926), 303.

[32] Cited by Helena Mennie Shire in *Song, Dance and Poetry of the Court of Scotland under King James VI* (Cambridge University Press, 1969), 86.

[33] Translated by Catherine Curtis, "The Social and Political Thought of Juan Luis Vives," in *A Companion to Juan Luis Vives*, ed. Charles Fantazzi (Brill, 2008), 143fn54.

[34] Sermon at Dexter Avenue Baptist Church, April 4, 1954. The Martin Luther King, Jr. Research and Education Institute makes public his speeches and sermons: http://kingen cyclopedia.stanford.edu/.

[35] *Richard III* (1.1.1). "I Have a Dream," address at the March on Washington for Jobs and Freedom (August 28, 1963).

[36] "Keep Moving from This Mountain," address at Spelman College (April 10, 1960).

dom, helping us reach our fullest capacities to make by emulating aspirational models, stretching our thinking as well as our words. Anything else is a curtailment of our birthright. As King paraphrased Shakespeare:

> '[H]e who filches from me my freedom robs me of that which not enriches him, but makes me poor indeed.' There is something in the soul that cries out for freedom.[37]

[37] *Othello* (3.3.157–59); "The Birth of a New Nation," sermon delivered at Dexter Avenue Baptist Church (April 7, 1957).

Donna Ruff, *Grrl Talk* (2004). Laser prints, ink, books. Private collection.

KINSMEN OF THE SHELF

The greatest part of a writer's time is spent in reading, in order
to write; a man will turn over half a library to make one book.
——Samuel Johnson, in *Boswell's Life* (1791)

Readers in Shakespeare's era were overwhelmed by *so many books
that we do not have time to read even the titles.*[1]

Seeking refuge from *too much to know,*[2] they made all kinds of
shortcuts to knowledge: anthologies, chrestomathies, commentaries, compendia, dictionaries, encyclopedias, epitomes, florilegia,
glossaries. Writers lifted from these digests, making it hard to
verify whether entire works were ever read. Shakespeare seems to
have cribbed liberally from Thomas Cooper's *Thesaurus* (1565),
a.k.a. treasury of words.

These shortcuts were *manuals*, guidebooks designed to be
"handy": both practical (for handwork) and portable (at hand).
As James Sanford's *The Manuell of Epictetus* (1567) glosses his title:

This booke (gentle Reader) is entituled a Manuell, which is de-
riued of the Latin word *Manuale*, and in Greeke is called *Enchy-
ridion*, bicause he may be contained ε υ χ ε ι ρ ι that is, in the hand.
It is a diminutiue of *Manus*, as it were a storehouse, & which
ought always to be had in hand, as the handle in the sword.

[1] Antonfrancesco Doni (1550), cited by Geoff Nunberg, "The Organization of Knowledge," *History of Information i218* (February 18, 2010): http://courses.ischool.berkeley
.edu/i218/s12/SLIDES/COFIKnowlM13-12GNb.pdf.
[2] Ann Blair lifts this line from *Love's Labor's Lost* (1.1.93) to title her study of responses
to information overload: *Too Much to Know: Managing Scholarly Information before the
Modern Age* (Yale University Press, 2010).

Yet as Renaissance educational handbooks were revised, they had a tendency to proliferate. (Little has changed in the business of textbook publishing!) For instance, the first edition of Erasmus's *Adagia*, or "sayings," gathered 818 proverbs and glosses; its final edition had swollen to 4,151. To paraphrase Pascal, it's harder to compose something short than something long.[3]

I want *How to Think like Shakespeare* to be handy—in the words of sweet Prince, *a handbook for the brilliant community.*[4] So here are some of the writers who have helped me sharpen my own thoughts. With Emily Dickinson, *I thank these Kinsmen of the Shelf.*[5]

1. OF THINKING

Hannah Arendt distinguishes among thinking, knowledge, and judgment, voicing the guarded hope that thinking might *prevent catastrophes, at least for myself, in the rare moments when the chips are down.*[6] My favorite line from Arendt's troubling teacher Martin Heidegger comes from the lecture "What Is Called Thinking?" (1952): *Perhaps thinking, too, is just something like building a cabinet. At any rate, it is a craft, a "handicraft."*

John Dewey's *How We Think* (1910) is widely cited, but I find his prose turgid. Mary Carruthers's *The Craft of Thought* (1998) demonstrates how *people do not "have" ideas, they "make" them.* Arthur Schopenhauer's chapter "On Thinking for Oneself" (1851) casts a skeptical eye on too much reading, citing Alexander Pope's *Dunciad: For ever reading, never to be read!* (3.194).

Cognitive studies of reading sometimes promise easy answers,

---

[3] *I have not made this longer than the rest [of my letters], but that I had not the leisure to make it shorter than it is.*
1658 English translation, cited by Quote Investigator, a.k.a. Garson O'Toole, whose website I've often gratefully consulted: https://quoteinvestigator.com.

[4] Dan Piepenbring, "The Book of Prince," *New Yorker*, September 9, 2019.

[5] "Unto my Books—so good to turn" (J604, Fr512), Houghton Library—(383c): https://www.edickinson.org/editions/1/image_sets/235782.

[6] "Thinking and Moral Considerations," *Social Research* 38, no. 3 (Autumn 1971): 446.

but work by Amy Cook, Mary Thomas Crane, Philip Davis, Arthur Kinney, Raphael Lyne, William Poole, and Lyn Tribble evades mechanistic temptations. Lyne maintains a useful blog, *What Literature Knows about Your Brain*:

https://www.english.cam.ac.uk/research/cogblog/

Barry Edelstein, Julia Lupton, A. D. Nuttall, and Michael Witmore have all considered Shakespearean thinking, via drama, political theology, philosophy, and metaphysics. Susan Stewart's *The Poet's Freedom* (2011) and Reginald Gibbons's *How Poems Think* (2016) are worth the while.

T. W. Baldwin's exhaustive study *Small Latine & Lesse Greeke* (1944) is still the source for Shakespeare's reading (since augmented by Leonard Barkan, Jonathan Bate, Colin Burrow, Stuart Gillespie, Charles Martindale, Robert Miola, and Leah Whittington). For an enthralling introduction to Shakespeare's favorite contemporaneous writer, check out Sarah Bakewell's *How to Live, or a Life of Montaigne in One Question and Twenty Attempts at an Answer* (2010).

Many have pondered how Shakespeare could *make the reader think*, and *learn the full powers of the English language.*[7] James Shapiro's *Shakespeare in America* (2014) and Theodore Leinwand's *The Great William: Writers Reading Shakespeare* (2016) compile such responses. Emma Smith explores *the ways in which Shakespeare's plays are spacious texts to think with* in *This Is Shakespeare* (2019).

Scientists discussing their thinking process include Conrad Hal Waddington's *Tools for Thought* (1977), David J. Helfand's *A Survival Guide to the Misinformation Age* (2016), and Jack Oliver's *The Incomplete Guide to the Art of Discovery* (1991), whose mantra is

---

[7] Samuel Taylor Coleridge, *Lectures on Shakespeare (1811–1819)*, ed. Adam Roberts (Edinburgh University Press, 2016), 32; Thomas Jefferson to Benjamin Moore, c. 1764, enclosed in Jefferson to John Minor, Monticello, August 30, 1814, in Paul Leicester Ford, ed., *The Writings of Thomas Jefferson* (G. P. Putnam's Sons, 1892–99), 11:424–25.

To discover, act like a discoverer. Thomas Wynn and Frederick L. Coolidge's *How to Think Like a Neandertal* (2013) blends paleontology with speculation about early craft practices and tool use.

Like Arthur Koestler's *The Act of Creation* (1964), Robert and Michèle Root-Bernstein's *Sparks of Genius* (2009) ranges across eras and disciplines. Charles P. Curtis, Jr., and Ferris Greenslet's *The Practical Cogitator; or, The Thinker's Anthology* (1945; 1983) would be a fine desert island book. Maria Popova's *Brainpickings* blog gleans stimulating excerpts from thought-filled makers.

2. OF ENDS

If I could assign just one essay to be read by every educator, legislator, student, and parent, it would be "The Tyranny of Three Ideas," the prologue to E. D. Hirsch's *Why Knowledge Matters* (2016):

http://hepg.org/HEPG/media/Documents/Introductions
/Hirsch_Why-Knowledge-Matters_Prologue.pdf?ext=.pdf

Hirsch, wrongly maligned as a reactionary, makes the progressive case that access to knowledge and vocabulary is a civil rights issue.

Jonathan Kozol's *Savage Inequalities* (1991) repudiates the fantasy that any school can bootstrap itself to "excellence" with just the right effort, just the right teachers, just the right curriculum, just the right assessment, just the right technology, just the right management, just the right . . . *anything* but the amelioration of poverty. Noliwe Rooks, *Cutting School* (2017), shows how racial and class disparities have been exacerbated by top-down reforms. Johann Neem's *Democracy's Schools* (2017) surveys the history of public education to better gauge its future.

Having once advocated for national testing schemes, Diane Ravitch is now among their most outspoken critics. Nicholas Tampio details the effects of accountability mania in *Common Core* (2018). Jerry Z. Muller's *The Tyranny of Metrics* (2018) assesses how obsessed we are with assessment. Audrey Watters's *Teaching Machines* (2020) records the long-standing desire to mechanize learning.

For a takedown of "scientific management," including evidence that Frederick Winslow Taylor fabricated data, see Matthew Stewart's *The Management Myth* (2009).

Daisy Christodoulou provides a welcome corrective in *Seven Myths about Education* (2014), as does David Didau, *What If Everything You Knew about Education Was Wrong?* (2015). Contrarian takes help bring into focus what's good about school; some of my favorites are Alexander Meiklejohn, *The Experimental College* (1928); Dorothy Sayers, *The Lost Tools of Learning* (1947); Paul Goodman, *Compulsory Mis-Education and the Community of Scholars* (1964); and Ivan Illich, *Deschooling Society* (1970).

I admire Alasdair MacIntyre's explorations of incommensurate ends in today's world, including his insistence that *teaching itself is not a practice, but a set of skills and habits put to the service of a variety of practices.*[8]

George Puttenham has fun "English"ing classical tropes in *The Arte of English Poesie* (1589). *The Forest of Rhetoric* catalogs over four hundred rhetorical figures:

http://rhetoric.byu.edu

Rhetoric: The Art of Persuasion, by Adina Arvatu and Andrew Aberdein (2015) is part of the charming Wooden Books series:

http://www.woodenbooks.com

3. OF CRAFT

Matthew Crawford, David Esterly, Peter Korn, Pamela Long, Juliette MacDonald, Karl Polyani, Richard Sennett, Pamela

---

[8] See his dialogue with Joseph Dunne, *Journal of Philosophy of Education* 36, no. 1 (2002): 1–19.

Smith, and Elspeth Whitney have all shaped my thinking about craft. A good place to start is Tanya Harrod's anthology *Craft* (2018). Alexander Langlands's *Cræft* (2018) recounts how he has revived artisanal practices. Doug Stowe's blog *Wisdom of the Hands* connects woodworking to children's intellectual development:

http://wisdomofhands.blogspot.com

I dare you not to cry at the gentle mastery of a one-room schoolhouse teacher in the documentary *To Be and to Have* (2002). Though it might seem to have little overt connection to education, the documentary *Jiro Dreams of Sushi* (2011) models craft in practice.

4. OF FIT

Mike Redwood's *Gloves and Glovemaking* (2016) explores the history of England's glovers. Robert Geddes's *Fit: An Architect's Manifesto* (2012) is admirably slim. On weaving as a figure for poetics, marriage, and political statecraft, see John Scheid and Jesper Svenbro, *The Craft of Zeus* (1996).

5. OF PLACE

Christopher Alexander reminds us why human-scaled places matter. Start with *A Pattern Language* (1977) and learn why we yearn for "light on two sides" of any room. Then move on to *The Nature of Order* (2003), which presents nothing less than a new cosmology. Edward Casey's work has inspired a generation of thinking about "getting back to place." On school as *skhole*, see Josef Pieper, *Leisure the Basis of Culture* (1948), and David C. Hutchison, *A Natural History of Place in Education* (2004). Frances Yates's *The Art of Memory* (1966) reconstructs the places/*loci* method.

6. OF ATTENTION

Many have written on the overreach of the attention industry, including Joshua Cohen, Richard Lanham, Jenny Odell, Caleb Smith, James Williams, Maryanne Wolf, and Timothy Wu. For an impassioned argument that we ought to preserve attention as a "commons," just as we preserve (or used to preserve!) air and water as a commons, see Matthew Crawford's *The World beyond Your Head* (2014). As early as 1971, Nobel economist Herbert Simon recognized the asymmetrical relationship between information overload and our finite capacities for attention. Mihaly Csikszentmihalyi popularized the psychology of optimal experience in *Flow* (1990)—the kind of immersive focus we ought to be preserving for our children. William James's *Talks to Teachers* (1899) underlines the need for attentive practices in education.

7. OF TECHNOLOGY

Jacques Ellul pushed us to comprehend how "technology" goes far beyond the latest electronic gadget. Inspired by Ellul, Donald Phillip Verene inquires, "Does Online Education Rest on a Mistake?" and answers, "It does."[9] Ursula Franklin, *The Real World of Technology* (1999), reveals technology as practice and structure, not just objects, making a distinction between holistic and prescriptive technologies.

This blog (whose owner I haven't been able to discern) alternates between inspiring me and making me despair:

http://www.digitalcounterrevolution.co.uk

As does James Bridle's *The New Dark Age* (2018):

We find ourselves today connected to vast repositories of knowledge and yet we have not learned to think. In fact, the opposite is

[9] *Academic Questions* 26 (2013).

true: that which was intended to enlighten the world in practice darkens it. . . . We only have to think, and think again, and keep thinking.

8. OF IMITATION

Do read Emerson's "Quotation and Originality," as well as Seneca's letter 84 to Lucilius, which sweetened the already long-established "bee" simile. For imitation and "double translation," see Roger Ascham's *The Schoolemaster* (1570). Donna Gorrell applies these practices to contemporary pedagogy in "Freedom to Write—through Imitation" (1987):

> https://wac.colostate.edu/jbw/v6n2/gorrell.pdf

As Neil Herz once pointed out, schools have been caught copying other schools' guidelines against plagiarism! Thomas Mallon's *Stolen Words* (1989) and Robert Shore's *Beg, Steal, and Borrow: Artists against Originality* (2018) both explore aesthetic practices; Austin Kleon's *Steal like an Artist* (2012) helps you put these practices into practice. John Kerrigan provides a graceful history in *Shakespeare's Originality* (2018). As Colin Burrow's *Imitating Authors: Plato to Futurity* (2019) promises to be exhaustive, I'm relieved that it didn't appear in time for me to emulate it. And I swear I didn't discover Gregory Roper's *The Writer's Workshop: Imitating Your Way to Better Writing* (2007) until after I had drafted my thoughts—great minds think alike, and so do we.

9. OF EXERCISES

A translation of the *Progymnasmata* can be found in G. A. Kennedy, *Progymnasmata: Greek Textbooks of Prose Composition and Rhetoric* (2003). Nick Wells provides a modern analogue of the *Progymnasmata* in "How to Teach like an Elizabethan Champion" (playing off of Lemov's *Teach like a Champion* [2010]):

https://englishremnantworld.wordpress.com/how-to-teach-like
-an-elizabethan-champion/

J. David Fleming urges us to revive this comprehensive rhetorical program. Cathy Birkenstein and Gerald Graff's *They Say/I Say*
(2005) offers a template-driven approach to composition; less
formulaic is Alastair Fowler's *How to Write* (2006).

10. OF CONVERSATION

At just the right moment, I was introduced to Stanley Cavell's
philosophy, which takes "conversation" as a figure for thinking
together about community, politics, and the world. His *Pursuits
of Happiness* (1984) is best read alongside a viewing of Holly-
wood remarriage comedies and their *unrehearsed intellectual
adventure.*[10]

Across the two volumes of *The Concept of Conversation* (2018–
19), David Randall traces this idea, from Cicero's *Sermo* to the
Enlightenment. Stephen Miller's *Conversation: A History of a Declining Art* (2006) covers a somewhat longer arc, from Plato to
today, and more anecdotally. Celeste Headlee's *We Need to Talk*
(2017) offers practical steps to recover this art.

11. OF STOCK

I prefer "stock" to the unhelpfully fraught word "tradition," the
scorn for which T. S. Eliot already noted a century ago: *Seldom,
perhaps, does the word appear except in a phrase of censure* ("Tradition and the Individual Talent" [1921]). Seth Lerer's *Tradition*
(2016) addresses the notion's legacy in literary studies. For "Invention," see Roland Greene's chapter in *Five Words: Critical Seman-
tics in the Age of Shakespeare and Cervantes* (2013).

---

[10] Michael Oakeshott, "The Voice of Poetry in the Conversation of Mankind," in *Ratio-
nalism in Politics and Other Essays* (Methuen, 1962), 198.

There's an entire library on "what the internet is doing to our brains" (Nicholas Carr); on the devaluation of "stock," see William Poundstone, *Head in the Cloud: Why Knowing Things Still Matters When Facts Are So Easy to Look Up* (2017), and Sam Wineburg, *Why Learn History (When It's Already on Your Phone)* (2018). While written about television, George W. S. Trow's *Within the Context of No Context* (1980) speaks to our moment: *Hell is where nothing connects with nothing.*[11]

12. OF CONSTRAINT

Here again I'd recommend Christopher Alexander's *A Pattern Language*, about working within limits—or, better, thinking of them not as limits, but as enabling infrastructure. *On Growth and Form* (1917) is a study by mathematical biologist D'Arcy Wentworth Thompson; more accessible is Philip Ball's *Patterns in Nature: Why the Natural World Looks the Way It Does* (2013). For thinking about constraints on an everyday basis, see *A Beautiful Constraint* (2015) by Adam Morgan and Mark Barden. John Elster's study *Ulysses and the Sirens* (1979; 1984) and its sequel *Ulysses Unbound* (2000) examine beneficial constraints from the perspective of social science.

13. OF MAKING

Eavan Boland and Mark Strand collaborated on *The Making of a Poem* (2001), an anthology of traditional forms. Unwittingly, I gathered many of the same quotations that Edward Hirsch cites in his chapter "Poet as Maker," found in his lovely *Poet's Choice* (2006). Peter Dormer's *The Art of the Maker* (1994) is clear-eyed, and accords with David Pye's *The Nature and Art of Workmanship*

---

[11] Vartan Gregorian, interviewed by Paola Alexander, *Arts Review* 3, no. 2 (1985): 6. Gregorian attributes this to Eliot's writing on Dante, but he seems to have massaged a line from *The Waste Land*: "I can connect / Nothing with nothing" (301–2).

(1968). The BBC/British Museum *History of World in 100 Objects* examines the kind of thinking that goes into making. The "Maker Movement" has made many manifestos (e.g., those of Chris Anderson and Mark Hatch), as well as produced online educational resources, suggestions for makerspaces, and the like; most are STEM-fixated. For a critique of the (often gendered) fetishization of *making* over less glamorous practices of *cultivating* and *maintaining*, see Debbie Chachra's "Why I Am Not a Maker," *Atlantic*, January 23, 2015. Pamela Smith leads *The Making and Knowing Project*, recovering reciprocal relations between craft and science:

https://www.makingandknowing.org

14. OF FREEDOM

Tom Hodgkinson's *How to Be Free* (2007) is a self-help book with the jauntiness of a Shakespearean play; a selection of Epictetus's Stoicism can be found in a short edition with the same title (2018). Ewan Fernie, Stephen Greenblatt, and Paul Kottman have written on Shakespeare and freedom. Earl Shorris founded the Clemente Course in the Humanities, recounted in *Riches for the Poor* (2000) and *The Art of Freedom: Teaching the Humanities to the Poor* (2013). Bruce Kimball's *Orators & Philosophers* (1995) narrates debates surrounding liberal education; his *The Liberal Arts Tradition: A Documentary History* (2010) lays out the primary sources, so you can converse with them yourself.

Gua Tewet with its "Tree of life," displaying hand stencils of men and women; from Luc-Henri Fage, *Borneo, Memory of the Caves* (1999). Creative Commons CC.

THANKS AND THANKS

Thinking and thanking in our language are words from one and the same source. Whoever follows out their meaning enters the semantic field of: "recollect," "bear in mind," "remembrance," "devotion." Permit me, from this standpoint, to thank you.
—Paul Celan, Bremen Prize acceptance speech (1958)

The first lesson in Shakespeare's Latin textbook included *amo magistrum*: "I love the master."[1] We are wary of the language of *mastery* today; for us, it connotes the devastating legacy of slavery. (A less loaded synonym: *virtuosity*.) Yet there are other, older forms of mastery, derived not from the capricious exercise of power, but rather from wisdom achieved over time. I trust that this book, the product of a long apprenticeship, serves as partial thanks for this (now contrarian) premise.[2]

In addition to scores of primary, secondary, college, and graduate school instructors who embodied thinking for me, I'm blessed to come from a family of teachers. My paternal grandfather taught in a one-room schoolhouse before becoming superintendent of his rural county's district; my maternal grandfather was named Minnesota's first teacher of the year in 1964; my dad won multiple teaching awards as a university professor. Aunts, uncles, cousins,

[1] William Lily's *A Shorte Introduction of Grammar* (1549), cited by Lynn Enterline in *Shakespeare's Schoolroom* (University of Pennsylvania Press, 2012), 24, 64.
[2] The title of my acknowledgments is drawn from *Twelfth Night* (3.3.14–15). My former student Mya Gosling's comic *Good Tickle Brain* discusses the history of editing this line, "And Ever Thanks?" (November 24, 2016): https://goodticklebrain.com/home/2016/11/24/and-ever-thanks.

in-laws, classmates, friends, and neighbors have all devoted their
lives to being forges for thought.

Conversations leading to this book were sustained by *delightful
playgrounds of the spirit*:[3] Yale University (Todd Gilman, Tom
Hyry, María Rosa Menocal, Alice Prochaska, and Timothy
Young); the University of Alabama (Sharon O'Dair); the Kenneth
Burke Society (David Blakesley, Bryan Crable, and Theon Hill);
Centre College (Mark Rasmussen and Philip White); "What's the
Word?" (Jonathan Gil Harris, Scott Maisano, and Sally Placksin);
the Meeman Center (John Rone, Susan Satterfield, and Geoff
Bakewell); Bard College–Berlin (Catherine Toal); The Center
School (Jon Greenberg); Agnes Scott College (Charlotte Artese
and James Diedrick); British Studies at Oxford (Michael Leslie);
the National Humanities Alliance (Stephen Kidd and Duane
Webster); the Shakespeare Institute (Peter Holland, Hester Lees-
Jeffries, Mary Polito, James Siemon, and Brian Walsh); the Uni-
versity of South Florida Sarasota–Manatee (Valerie Lipscomb and
Jonathan Scott Perry); the National Humanities Center (Sarah
Beckwith, Maria Fahey, Geoffrey Harpham, and Donovan Sher-
man); Phi Beta Kappa (John Churchill); Mississippi State Univer-
sity (Tommy Anderson and Chris Snyder); Southwestern Univer-
sity (Ed Burger and Michael Saenger); Proof School (Ian Brown
and Paul Zeitz); Opera Memphis (Ned Canty); Beth Sholom
Lehrhaus (Jonathan Judaken and Daniel Unowsky); Humanities
Tennessee (Timothy Henderson); the University of Mississippi
(Ivo Kamps, Karen Raber, Jason Solinger, and Joseph Ward); the
College of St. Scholastica (James Crane, Shelley Gruskin, Bill Ho-
dapp, and Stephanie Johnson); Great Hearts Academies (John
Briggs, Scott Crider, Robert Jackson, Koos van Leeuwen, and
Gregory Roper); Big Beacon Radio (Dave Goldberg); Shake-

---

[3] John Amos Comenius, cited by John Edward Sadler in *J. A. Comenius and the Concept
of Universal Education* (Barnes and Noble, 1966), 209.

speare's Globe (Farah Karim-Cooper and Will Tosh); Austin College (Max Grober, Marjorie Hass, Dan Nuckols, and Will Radke); Dickinson College (Carol Ann Johnston, Margaret Mauer, and Jacob Sider Jost); the University of Lausanne (Lukas Erne, Kader Hegedüs, Rachel Nisbet, and Kirsten Stirling); the University of Geneva (Aleida Auld, Lukas Erne, Oliver Morgan, Maria Shmygol, and Devani Singh); Grinnell College (Louis Jenkins and Ellen Mease); The Morgan Library (John Marciari); Libertas School of Memphis (the entire faculty and staff!); Rhodes Faculty Lair (Noelle Chaddock, Timothy Huebner, David Rupke, and Betsy Sanders); the West Tennessee State Penitentiary (Stephen Haynes and all of the students); the University of Zurich (Elisabeth Bronfen, Philip Sarasin, and Barbara Straumann); the Shakespeare Association of America (Anston Bosman, Marjorie Garber, John Guillory, Heather James, Natasha Korda, Jeffrey Masten, Carla Mazzio, Lena Cowen Orlin, and Dyani Johns Taff); Rhodes Summer School in London (Vanessa Rogers); the Ohio Valley Shakespeare Conference (Russell Bodi, Timothy Francisco, Philip Goldfarb Styrt, Carol Mejia LaPerle, Jimmy Newlin, and Nate Smith); the University of Dallas (Kathryn Davis, Jonathan Malesic, Andrew Moran, Stefan Novinski, Gregory Roper, Will Roudabush, and Christopher Schmidt); the University of St. Thomas (Michael Boler, Clinton Brand, Christopher Evans, Janet Lowery, and Samuel Shehadeh); the University of Tennessee–Chattanooga (Bryan Hampton, Joseph Jordan, Devori Kimbro, Emily Lindner, Aaron Shaheen, and Carl Springer); Marymount University (Tonya-Marie Howe and Marguerite Rippy); the Warburg Institute (Brian Chalk, William Engel, Andrew Hiscock, Rory Loughnane, Peter Sherlock, Bill Sherman, and Grant Williams); and the Folger Shakespeare Library (Rachel Dankert, LuEllen DeHaven, Ross Duffin, Marissa Greenberg, Amanda Herbert, Rosalind Larry, Kathleen Lynch, Sara Pennell, Camille Seerattan, Abbie Weinberg, Owen Williams, and most of all Mike Witmore).

Earlier trials appeared in *Inside Higher Ed*; *Chapter 16*; the *Chronicle of Higher Education*; *Perfect Duluth Day*; *The Routledge Research Companion to Shakespeare and Classical Literature*; *The Oxford Handbook of Shakespeare and Performance*; and *Teaching the Literature Survey*. My words were honed by Scott Jaschik; Margaret Renkl; Alex Kafka; Paul Lundgren; Sean Keilen and Nick Moschovakis; James Bulman; and Gwynn Dujardin, James Lang, and John Staunton. I've been inspired by readers who shared their own anxieties and aspirations about education.

Rhodes College provided me a platform for thinking about Shakespeare, whether in classrooms, with fellow teachers, at board meetings, or among visitors hosted through the Pearce Shakespeare Endowment. I never had the pleasure of meeting Dr. Iris Annette Pearce, but her bequest has enriched conversations for thousands of Memphians, myself most of all. I remain grateful that the stewardship of her gift was entrusted to me by my Rhodes English Department colleagues, all of whom have helped temper my thoughts. Lori Garner kept me from straying too far in etymology, as did Patrick Gray in theology, Tim Huebner in citizenship, Seth Rudy in wit, Susan Satterfield in Latin, Caki Wilkinson in poetics, and Lorie Yearwood in receipts. At the Barret Library, Darlene Brooks, Rachel Fineman, Amanda Ford, Marci Hendrix, Kenan Padgett, and the irrepressible Bill Short harvested stock for my inventory. Bob Entzminger, Brian Shaffer, Jenny Brady, and the ever-*exigeant* Michael Leslie all make dead wood more blest than living lips. My prose has been beautified with Mike's feathers; he merits credit as a tacit editor.

My parents first taught me how to think (much as they might sometimes regret the consequences!).

Tim Blackburn first taught me how to think like Shakespeare.

Scott Samuelson once chided me with a poem affectionately titled "On the Necessity of Footnotes." For three decades, he has inspired me to make the proper annotation to *animae dimidium meae*.[4]

As Rebecca Solnit discerned:

> Thinking is generally thought of as doing nothing in a production-oriented culture, and doing nothing is hard to do. It's best done by disguising it as doing something, and the something closest to doing nothing is walking.[5]

Much of this book was hashed out while I was doing nothing with Peter Lund and Todd Sample.

Catherine Toal's quick (and quick-witted) readings made me believe that this was a real book.

John Guillory encouraged me to *never apologize for what we do, just explain it clearly and positively*. I'm sorry if I've—wait, I take that back!

At last I can reciprocate the sign of my crafty collaborator Ayanna Thompson: YOU ROCK.

Jim and Taryn Spake gave me a room—really, a whole cabin—of one's own.

Bob and Sara Nardo showed me *libertas* in practice.

Danny Kraft more than lived up to his surname.

Margot Studts cheered me past the finish line.

In the beginning was the conversation: I thank Claudia and Larry Allums, Florence Amamoto, John Andrews, Sarah Bakewell, Burlin Barr, Emiliano Battista, David Beard, Roger Berkowitz, Claude Brew, Leslie Brisman, David Bromwich, Vinessa Brown, Jennifer Bryan, Phil Bryant, Richard Burt, Michael Cavanagh, Stanley Cavell, Thad Cockrill, Neal Colton, John Curry, David Dault, Chris Davis, Brent Dexter, Elizabeth Dobbs, Michelle Dowd, Jerry Duncan, Mark Edington, Eric Eliason, Sarah Enloe,

[4] *half of my soul*, Horace, *Carmina* (1.3.8); see also Marc Bloch, "To Lucien Febvre," in *The Historian's Craft*, trans. Peter Putnam (1954; Manchester University Press, 1984), 2.
[5] *Wanderlust: A History of Walking* (Penguin, 2005), 5.

Cookie Ewing, Deborah Forsman, Cary Fowler, Bill Germano, Richard Gibson, Leonard Gill, Joe Gordon, Heidi and Matt Graham, Austin Grimes, Charles Hacker, Donal Harris, Ben Harth, Don Hirsch, Sarit Horwitz, Nick Hutchison, Alan Jacobs, Andre and Dorothy Jones, Mike Judge, Peter Kalliney, Andrew Keener, John Kenney, Robert Khayat, Timothy Kirchner, Elizabeth Knoll, David Kotok, Mitch and Nivine Kotok, Rachel Kotok, Jonathan Lamb, John Latimer, Elise and Preston Lauterbach, Margaret Litvin, Alan Liu, Bob Llewellyn, Jill Locke, Julia Lupton, Jamie MacDougall, Karen Marsalek, John McGee, Katie McGee, Scott McMillin, Chris Mills, Daniel Morgan, Thomas Moore, Will Murray, Johann Neem, Jim Nephew, Charlie Newman, Peter Nilsson, Donal O'Shea, Gene Palumbo, Suzie Park, Andrew Parker, Geo Poor, Rachel Potek, Bill Pritchard, Ray Privett, Sharon Prizant, David Randall, Jonathan Rees, Jessica Richard, Michael Roth, Aaron Rubinstein, Abe Schacter-Gampel, Christine Schlesinger, James Shapiro, Russell Shapiro, Marc Shell, Jamie Sirico, Emma Smith, Michael St. Thomas, Joyce Sutphen, Michael Swanlund, Brian Thompson, Henry Turner, Krista Twu, Greg Vanderheiden, Helen Vendler, Eric Vrooman, Josh Waxman, Robert Watson, C. C. Wharram, Bronwen Wickkiser, Daniel Williams, and countless former students who have helped me articulate why we do this.

Princeton University Press has been *wisdom's workshop* for me. Peter Dougherty made it happen. Anne Savarese was alternately prodding and patient, in measure even. She solicited readers who were sympathetic to this idiosyncratic project. Dimitri Karetnikov thought through the images with me. Lauren Lepow's keen mind made her the ideal copyeditor. Lorraine Doneker finessed this finicky format. Brigid Ackerman, Lisa Black, Claudia Classon, Katie Lewis, Jodi Price, Laurie Schlesinger, and Jenny Tan all graciously fielded my ceaseless queries.

In untold and unanticipated ways, becoming a parent at first unsettled, but eventually trued what I thought about education.

I'm indebted to Ruth Lillian, Axel Felix, and Pearl Jeanne, all three restless thinkers. Like Timon's painter, they persistently inquired, *Papa, when comes your book forth?*[6] Thank you for being patient!

I dedicate this work to long-suffering Sarah: your *meet and happy conversation is the chiefest and the noblest end.*

[6] *Timon of Athens* (1.1.27).

Printer's mark, Edmund Spenser, *Complaints* (London, 1591).

INDEX

An Author ought to make the Index to his book, whereas
the book itself may be written by any person else.
—Nicolás Antonio, *Bibliotheca Hispana sive Hispanorum* (1672)

O'Hara, Frank, 11
O'Toole, Garson, 154
Oakeshott, Michael, 50, 52, 161
Odell, Jenny, 158
Ogilvy, David, 123n17
Oliver, Jack, 155
Oliver, Mary, xiii
Ording, Philip, 95n36
originality, 74–77, 79, 82, 150, 160.
    See also plagiarism
Ortega y Gasset, José, 56, 86
Orwell, George, xiv, 50, 95
Osiris, myth of, xv
ostomachion puzzle, viii, xiv–xv
Ovid, 73, 79–80, 107–10

Paine, Thomas, xii n12
Palladio, Andrea, 42n22
paradox, 101, 121, 123; sorites, 66,
    70; Zeno's, 16
Parmenides, 114
Pasanek, Brad, 31n14
Pascal, Blaise, 154
past, engaging with the, ix, xii,
    11, 13, 32, 52, 77, 100, 103,
    112, 116–17, 144, 146, 148,
    150
patchwork, xiii, 115
Pater, Walter, 115
patterns, xv, 7, 23, 27, 32, 81, 122,
    158, 162
Paz, Octavio, 33
Peele, George, 38
Pepin, Jacques, 88
periodic table, 107
personalized learning (*sic*), 43, 61
Petrarch, Francesco, 52–53, 125
Philibert de Vienne, 10
piano, tuning of, 25–27

Picasso, Pablo, 103
Pickersgill, 54–56
Pieper, Josef, 158
pill, swallow a Shakespeare, 65n7
Pindar, 135
place, xiv, 33, 37, 40, 42, 45, 47–53,
    102, 124, 139, 158
plagiarism, 74–75, 117, 143, 160.
    See also originality
platforms, xiii, 68, 168
Plato, 2, 28, 70, 114
Plautus, 83, 104
playfulness, xii, 7n16, 51, 90–91, 95,
    123–24
Pliny the Elder, vii
Plutarch, 40n8, 73, 150
plyometrics, 85, 104
Polyani, Karl, 157
Poole, William, 155
Pope, Alexander, 8, 37–38, 77, 154
Popova, Maria, 156
Postman, Neil, x n6
Pound, Ezra, 80
Poundstone, William, 162
PowerPoint, 70–71, 91n26
practice, 4n8, 11, 16, 26–28, 31–33,
    44–45, 49, 53, 61, 75, 78–79, 82,
    87–88, 100, 104, 116, 134, 138,
    149, 157–60. *See also* exercises
Prince, 154
Progymnasmata, 86, 89, 141,
    160–61
Protopsaltis, Spiros, 49
proverbs, 9, 16, 37, 44, 67, 74, 138,
    150, 154
Pullman, Philip, 107
Pulter, Hester, 128
Puttenham, George, 28, 42–43, 87,
    157